The Business of America

Paths for the 21st Century

edited by Marcus Raskin

The Business of America:
How Consumers Have Replaced Citizens
and How We Can Reverse the Trend
Saul Landau

The Business of America

How Consumers Have Replaced Citizens and How We Can Reverse the Trend

Saul Landau

ROUTLEDGE
New York and London

Published in 2004 by
Routledge
29 W 35th Street
New York, NY 10001
www.routledge-ny.com

Published in Great Britain by
Routledge
11 New Fetter Lane
London EC4P 4EE
www.routledge.co.uk

Routledge is an imprint of the Taylor & Francis Group.
Printed in the United States of America on acid-free paper.
Typesetting: BookType

10 9 8 7 6 5 4 3 2 1

Library of Congress Cataloging-in-Publication Data

Landau, Saul.
  The business of America : how consumers have replaced citizens and how we can reverse the trend / Saul Landau.
    p. cm. — (Paths for the twenty-first century)
  ISBN 0-415-94468-6 (cloth) -- ISBN 0-415-94469-4 (pbk.)
  1. United States—Social conditions—1980– 2. Consumption (Economics)—United States. 3. Mass media—United States. 4. Air pollution—United States.
5. Corporations—Corrupt practices—United States. 6. Fraud—United States.
7. United States—Politics and government—2001– I. Title. II. Series.

  HN59.2.L36 2004
  306'.0973—dc22

                                                          2003025689

To all educators who,
often at great risk,
teach against oppression.

Contents

Series Editor's Preface

The aim of the *Paths for the 21st Century* series is to encourage new ways of looking at problems, to foster practical approaches to long-standing problems, and to promote the knowledge capable of positively influencing people's everyday lives. The books in this series are intended to give the powerless a greater role in the discourse that strengthens communities without creating barriers between these communities. To these ends the Paths Project seeks out new ways for future generations to evade the pitfalls of the twentieth century while fostering a spirit of liberation that focuses on dignity and decency for all people.

The Paths Project acknowledges three contending approaches to the use and function of knowledge. The first views knowledge and inquiry as primarily in the service of domination, control, and the manipulation of others. This form of knowledge most often results in a blind, unquestioning, and dogmatic faith. The second approach focuses on knowledge as merely utilitarian with an ever increasing focus on technical specializations and sub-specialization. It assumes a specific cause and solution to a given problem, and pays insufficient attention to the aims and values to which knowledge is ultimately subservient.

It is the third approach which I take as the basis for the Paths Projects. This approach assumes that knowledge and inquiry are directed toward liberation rather than control, seeking to understand the relationships between institutions, systems, problems and, most importantly, values. This approach ultimately fosters greater democratic discourse and a more progressive social reconstruction. The Paths Project presumes that this third approach affords us the insight and wisdom necessary for creating the conditions of dignity and equality and for ending the exploitation of one group over another.

Paths for the 21st Century seeks to draw together scholars and activists to create an invisible college, working together and trading ideas to stimulate thinking and discussion about issues affecting us domestically and internationally. It will present radical alternatives concerning what should be changed, and how these changes can be accomplished. In the end, the aim of the Paths Project is to lay the foundation for a new progressivism chastened by the lessons of the twentieth century and reconstructed for the twenty-first century. This is no small goal which, ultimately, in a democracy, can only be achieved through discussion and a community of inquiry and deliberation. It is my hope that the books in this series will help to begin and contribute to that dialogue without which social justice, personal freedom, and a progressive twenty-first century will never come about.

Marcus Raskin
Institute for Policy Studies

Foreword
Marcus Raskin

Shopping Culture or Rethinking Culture?

To use John Kennedy's phrase, Landau would probably say "Ich bin ein shopper!" But shopping takes time and contemporary America parcels out time as yet another product, indeed as the commercial way to link us to a present and future. What could be better than the 20 second commercials that tell us "all we need to know" about deodorants, cars, elixir pills, and Victoria's Secret?

The corporate and war making culture is linked to make, sell, discard, and destroy. The virtually instantaneous processing of information receives the highest form of approval, which enables members of the culture to kill—in so many forms. During the Cold War virtual destruction, war games, and other "playful" activities prepared the society for real destruction. During these decades, the government spent tens of billions on tens of thousands of scientists and technologists. They paid for a military apparatus that used their "creative" lives to decrease the amount of time the US needed to respond to a nuclear launch by an aggressor from 15 minutes to less than 7. This would allow the President to launch a preemptive strike. After living through this era of what C. Wright Mills called "crackpot realism," I read Landau's book in preparation for this introduction. I thought he had taken leave of his senses because he argued that culture had become shopping and marketing. Could culture have evolved or devolved into nothing but shopping?

Look at the symbiotic relationship between art collectors, museums, and the art market. Or at the process by which our most gifted minds invest their brains on research for weapons of mass destruction. Or those who use enormous artistic talent to make sophisticated ads to sell us drugs; some of our best doctors have also become salespeople for drug companies.

This is not a new revelation, but something has been added in recent decades. And this realization has caused me to worry about ideas we project about cultures of decency and dignity. To envision societies where creativity centers life requires us to confront the forces that will attempt to dominate the future.

The subliminal message in advertising as well as in the commercial products themselves attempts to obscure the very basis for a decent and creative culture by turning the cooperative and collective nature of people inside out.

Some new techniques in the psychology of marketing illustrate this idea. J B Watson's "pioneering" work on behavioral psychology for the Thompson ad agency has taken on a new feature: *neuromarketing*. According to the Bright House Institute for Thought Sciences which advises corporate clients such as Coca Cola and Pepperidge Farms on the "most advanced neuroscientific research capabilities and understanding of how the brain thinks, feels, and motivates behavior," this kind of knowledge enables corporations to "establish the foundation for loyal, long-lasting consumer relationships." Like snake oil salesmen of the past, Bright House promoters offer the elixir of life, meaning the tonic of perpetual consumer-corporate life.

Such a notion should ring the bells of absurdity, given how little even scientists know about the brain. But from "business logic," absurdity makes sense: re-program people—human nature—for a culture of perpetual shopping and label it "ultimate satisfaction."

This group of research scientists and businessmen faces rough seas in their attempts to dominate the culture of the future even though at least one university, Emory University, has become a willing party to this new "science." A group of psychologists, who understand the scholar's ethos, are trying to stop Emory University from being part of the new shopping science (UNDERNEWS, Sam Smith, December 1, 2003).

In the globalized world, culture loses its organic ties and becomes whatever is bought and sold—or stolen by one class from another. Culture loses authenticity and becomes exploitative.

Ironically, the new meaning of culture is apolitical. Its purpose is to reinforce the prevailing social system of oligarchy and capitalism. The assumption of this system is that the market place will fund the "best" art, architecture, music, and thus define the nature of society. But this is naïve.

Saul Landau, writer, filmmaker, poet, historian, and activist understands that culture is something to be consciously made; critical and political in the sense of plucking holes in the plastic shell that covers the lies, contradictions, and evasions of Authority. Culture relates to truths that become obvious once they are revealed. This understanding of culture becomes a battleground, not only of what is acceptable, different or avant-garde in the arts, but what is acceptable as a moral stance. Landau, the revolutionary, seeks a moral tableau in which societies may judge what they do and who they are. This is no easy task for his definition of culture includes movement away from the settled and towards the alternative. But most important, he has a reconstructive vision of how people should act one to another in order to make a decent, democratic culture.

But American society continues to struggle about what democracy means. And democracy can be as exploitive as any other system of government, especially when its mode of communication becomes incessant propaganda without critique.

Landau speaks of culture in unashamedly didactic forms. He does not separate politics from culture, nor do I. He does understand that great art in all of its manifestations can create a humane world consciousness, but one which includes cultural struggle. Landau even resembles those 19th Century dreamers who hoped that *bildungsroman* would build an understanding of decency and judgment.

He has no commitment to that European tradition that saw itself as the beginning and end of culture. Rather for him the culture is what people do in their creative, intentional, and unintentional ways; like a layered cake, integral and supported by one another.

Layerings in American culture (cultures) manifest themselves in the politics of the market, the attempts to hold on to social differences and class though consumption and shopping. Capitalism through oligopoly seeks to show differentiation and finally, the oneness of the system, identifying from many into one process and project in of all things—according to Landau—shopping.

When we report on the quick take, or see a commercial, or listen to the "headlines," and talk of preventive war, or when we walk down the street and see images which contradict and don't seem to fit together except that they are there, we are forced to consider the reality of how we live in the framework others have cobbled for us. Here Landau serves as a guide. Throughout his essays and activism Landau is making an analytic point. He is saying that in order to recenter ourselves we must be prepared to recognize the obvious. He calls us to differentiate, make judgments, and act to change oppressive social frameworks which may seem to be benign but whose benign purposes have vanished. This is the only way we can recenter ourselves and shape a culture beyond war and degradation and utopian illusion.

When we experience an event that we don't experience except through media Landau the filmmaker questions the authenticity of what we do not know except through images. This is his purpose in pursing a factual basis for culture—beyond the slick appearance and image. We are to make sense of social reality by denying the inauthentic one presented to us. And we have those who insist that all of life including our scientific knowledge is a social construction of reality no different from a movie. Others say that like a fake painting on top we know there is a truer picture underneath. The question is how to get to it and what to do about it when and if we find it. But do we have the time to look, to assess, indeed to deliberate? It would seem that modern culture has little room for deliberation. The advantage of the university had been the slack time, a time to think and wonder. But the modern university adopts the business quantitative standard of the bottom line and the professor soon learns that she is on an externally imposed assembly line.

You might ask the question what kind of person takes on the responsibility of analyzing the moment and the people who bring us that moment. It is likely that he also is a shopper, but a special kind, who peers into the windows of our lives. But what is he seeking? What are any of us looking for?

His bullet like essays tell us to stop sleepwalking and realize that reasonableness and rationality can occur if we are not blinded by light or the darkness of the flickering caves of television. We even may seek transformation and reconstruction in the hope that there is more than what we see, or more than what is given, or what we think we remember through the shorted circuits of our minds. Landau understands that media and war pummeling leave us with diminished cognitive and broken moral faculties. In every essay Landau wonders whether the capitalist realism of the marketplace and the war room defeated the culture of hope. Indeed, he seems to imply that the culture of hope is a weak reed. Is culture no more than the fashion of clothing in which we say "this goes with that" or for that matter, is culture of the conscious reduced to laughing at ignorant unjust and cynical men who specialize in seeking honor through defense of their oligarchy? It may not be all of culture but it is certainly a part of it. Oligarchs have their meaning of culture and it may be there in high art and criminal acts which they help to maintain either carelessly as F. Scott Fitzgerald put it or intentionally as CIA covert operators who act during the day as spies and robbers and attend art openings at night or wear the right insignia logo and clothes for war.

Landau's short takes, his mini essays, are only part of the story of re-appropriation of culture. If, as Landau would have it, culture is struggle, culture is also poetry. But poetry now has to adjust to the evanescent, the silliness of it all, the anger which doesn't come from personal pain of love or the beauty of nature or the fear of death. Now the poet has to deal with what is created by social, political, and economic institutions. And how to respond to them. A person loses his self, his inner core in modern western life. T.S. Eliot becomes a defender of reaction and a pessimist about man [sic] and the human spirit. There is for Eliot no other way. But one wonders whether Eliot's exhaustion and conservativism is nothing more than Marx's "dead hand of the past on us."

What does the poet wDuckho believes that poetry is the hard edge of the reality to do? He becomes a moralist demanding something else from humanity, that is to say, our culture. If the poet is also the moralist he is a judgment maker, a prophet, and sometimes a "besservisser" who gets under people's skin with his advice and claims of seeing beneath the fake painting. Plato understood the danger of poets; they were troublemakers and wanted them out of the city. Those who would stay had to sing in very specific keys outlined and enforced by the state, and later the Church, or the State—even the corporations. Plato sought stability and harmony but this is hardly the way of the artist who believes he is assigned the task of remaking the symbols of culture and therefore the culture itself. These battles are as old as the one which Michelangelo fought with the Church and Diego Rivera fought with Nelson Rockefeller.

We are not all poets and we may sing in the shower but this doesn't make us ready to perform at the Metropolitan Opera which stages the operatic canon at the expense of the new. So what happens to those who had ideals and purposes beyond the culture of shopping and consumption? What happens then? We have mortgages, responsibilities, and we have even hidden our doubts from ourselves.

What happens if all possibilities that we could choose or make are taken? What if "keeping up" and not "falling behind," smiling, being punctual, wearing a tie or not becomes our only good end, that is our culture? And that we are paid off with modern bread and circuses, shopping, politainment, and the choice of social evasion. In other words, suppose through globalization we organized ourselves into the hum drum and conventional where disease, starvation, and war remain but the culture of the traditional and our aspirations are buried and destroyed for no fault of our own. In that case, what disappears is not only the person but the aspiration, and we do not see the wormhole to crawl out of. Nor finally do we want to.

When he was chief economist at the World Bank, Lawrence Summers, now president of Harvard, said that Africa and the poorer nations should import the garbage created by the West, which no longer has room in its own dump, because economically it would amount to progress. During World War II, another former Harvard president, James Conant, counseled the use of nuclear weapons against the homes of Japanese workers as a means of inspiring terror and fear. Neither Summers, an economist, nor Conant, a chemist, laid claim to being moralists. They were, however, "educated." Justifications are invariably found for the wretched conditions from Dalits in India, to women slaves of the Sudan, to garbage scavengers of Cairo, to the millions destroyed in the Indo-China war. Landau cannot abide the injustice or the rationalization for it. Indeed, he has staked out the border between the United States and Mexico for a documentary trilogy about the depravity in our own midst.

A radical critique might of imperialism would say that culture itself is dying and the ghost of T.S. Eliot might even argue that no other way exists. But if we live without the possibilities of "redemption" or alternatives, then we are celebrating humanity's demise and we are getting drunk at a collective, universal wake. Of course not everyone is attending the same wake, although "globalization," that monstrous word, echoes with insistence that everyone must attend the wake served by class and cost differentiated products and the shopping network; unless you work in the sweatshops of Haiti, Pakistan, or Korea. Landau, the realist and the romantic, sees other truths.

Reconstruction and transformation undergird the work of the moralist and thus must recognize the power of this Goliath culture. Nevertheless, different cultures struggle to be born; others try to protect themselves. Layering aside, not everyone is going to be part of the same culture, the same values, the same assumptions. Nor does everyone in a particular culture hold the same values and assumptions.

In the American context when four young men refused to move from a white segregated soda fountain, this became a transcendent moment in American history and culture. The culture changed, what was permissible to say in public spaces changed.

Landau knows that throughout the world thousands of such examples enforce dignity, places where people say "no more indignity" and create the basis for freedom, whether through art, thought, even passion. More often than not, they occur in the ordinary world far from the power of the state. They represent the *creative* culture and criticism which personifies Landau and the work of the artist. What a curiosity those moments are, and how fixed they are in our memories. One question, and certainly not the only one, is how and whether a political system honors those transcendent moments, in the person.

In both cases the question is understanding and action beyond the moment as far as the individual is concerned. Landau understands that the task of the collectivity is far more complicated. A state may cause or encourage suffering. A collectivity may be fooled by leadership; it may not escape institutional forms that appear rational but are destructive. The collectivity may approve of a clean art which in fact masks and reinforces immobilism, passivity, and the filth of actual destruction. It will be an art which neither inspires, nor explains, nor helps. It may be a commercial art which fulfills our aspirations of happiness or patriotic nostalgia as in Norman Rockwell. But for the most part commercial art claims our happiness is to be found in products from Coca Cola, to automobiles, shaving lotion, and toothpaste. And it claims that this is the way to bring our personal fears together with our social selves. It may be the fascist and Nazi art of Hitler and Mussolini's time which sought purity and which highlighted Beethoven and Wagner in the death camps. They may be dominated by the kind of agitprop once found in Stalin's posters.

Multiculturalism in American society is not an empty word for it may either force or recognize the right of people to cross class, ethnic, and religious boundaries. What is the important lesson of *West Side Story*? It is the story of leftist artists who choose how love and music require crossing boundaries. It is in that kind of love that respect for the other is found. Now the struggle of modern culture is to bring this idea into reality. When we read, for example, the Universal Declaration of Human Rights or the covenants, we see they are based on the central conception that cultural rights are the fundamental problematic in modern life. Now this comes down in various ways.

The old imperial way occurred through domination, rape, and plunder. More recently imperialism also embodied Donald Duck, a cartoon symbol, intended to wipe out other people's cultures and national identities. It included occupation and it even includes technology transfer where the weaker nation must become "technological" buying equipment which hooks its society to an oil based international economy. So, if this is the colonizing way that old cultures are transcended, is there a reconstructive way? It is from artists, musicians, those expert in crafts, architects, writers, and filmmakers that a new culture of necessity will be born, one that contains more than what is critical in order to eat and have housing. The organizing of culture around housing, eating, art, and music could be comes from the everyday life of people. Over the time span of the twentieth century, there have been many examples of small magazines, blues and jazz, and other forms of music making folk life, and high art which were not captured by either the state or the marketplace. Small science labs formed and people with nothing more than paper and pencil unlocked the secrets of the universe. This kind of culture, which one may view as a culture of reconstruction, defiance, and self-definition, is the basis upon which culture can be sustained and perpetuated.

In this context, certain institutions that have national and international legitimacy can aid in developing an international culture. Thus for example, churches and universities can aid in developing an international culture. This was the original hope of the organizers of the United Nations Educational, Scientific, and Cultural Organization who saw culture as stemming from the realities of the world. The television and radio became important elements in transmitting this culture, just as the penny newspapers had a powerful effect as a dynamic of change, sometimes good, sometimes bad, so is the case that television and radio, locally controlled, hopefully can have a similar effect. With new forms of technology, cultures in cyberspace are now created. These cultures develop their own language and dialogue and appear to have their own purpose which is usually a positive one.

The organizing of a multicultural society in America which is linked in a positive way to liberation and humaneness transnationally can have a powerful effect in creating a world civilization with plural cultures. This will be one task of the twenty-first century as each group and culture wants to be recognized as an actor of history with its own dynamic. These actors would be expressed internationally quickly through television, radio, and computer. What is important once such recognition occurs, is that a core of values reflecting dignity and decency can be made operative throughout the world without resorting to using their obverse, namely coercion, war, and imperialism. Culture is by its nature sneaky and subversive, for it is through culture that those who are dominated, once they understand their power, can transform the dominator. It is through the analytic mind that we learn parallels and differences. And it is through moral action that we expose and bring to the table of relevance a new consciousness, and the possibilities of reconstruction. This Landau understands with his contribution to redefining political culture. His methods are like short outtakes in a film or radio commentary that tells a truth beyond itself. Each one tells us something and each one demands connection to a greater whole. Each one is a moral statement and every one demands dissection and linkage to ourselves, our condition, and the culture in which we want to live.

Acknowledgments

This book grew out of a request—nay a demand—that Marcus Raskin made: "You must write a critique of culture." So, ever obedient to one of the great moralists of our time, I began to write the essays. The fellows and staff of the Institute for Policy Studies inspired me. Their creativity, commitment to justice and truth, and their optimistic spirit, often in the face of dire reality, served as a motivating force. I also want to acknowledge my colleagues at the Transnational Institute in Amsterdam for continuing to stimulate me with their cutting-edge ideas.

Special thanks go to Farrah Hassen, the mother of all research assistants, and a fabulous editor as well, and to Rebecca Switzer, whose brilliant critical insights delight and amaze me. All my children and grandchildren contributed in one way or another to this work as well.

I am also indebted to *Progreso Weekly* (www.progresoweekly.com), the gritty zine published by brave Miami Cuban-Americans, *Counterpunch*, and *Znet* for publishing my essays in their original form. Some of these essays appeared in abbreviated form in America's most interesting weekly newspaper, *Anderson Valley Advertiser*.

I also owe Dr. Barbara Way, dean of the College of Letters, Arts, and Social Sciences at the California State Polytechnic University, Pomona, Technology Vice President Dr. Michael Berman, and especially Dr. Bob Suzuki, former Cal Poly President, for encouraging me to keep writing. Thanks as well to my colleagues and fellow union (CFA) brothers and sisters at Cal Poly for their continuous support.

Errors and stupidities belong exclusively to me, much as I would like to attribute such gaffes to others.

Introduction

Civic exhaustion is the biggest problem facing us.[1]
—Ralph Nader

Look at our culture of consumption as a scientist would see bacteria growing in an immense Petri dish. We develop or get conditioned amidst an amorphous atmosphere of perpetual sales pitches as if human nature itself possesses some compulsion to lure us, like the biblical serpent with its glowing apple did to Eve. Instead of having a simple protein, our culture dish contains sophisticated inorganic material from advertisers who promise to bring daily and eternal satisfaction to "you," the ever-needy individual, around whom the world revolves.

This "consumer" (who has replaced the citizen in popular commercial jargon) reacts emotionally as sales propagators desperately attempt to induce in him or her ever more shopping as the only acceptable universal behavior—one that will deal with material inadequacies and redeem the spirit as well.

According to researchers at Media Tank, a group founded by *Harper's* publisher John R. MacArthur and Janine Jackson from *Fairness and Accuracy in Reporting*, "The average person is exposed to more than 3600 commercial messages each day." The investigators compiled their data from newspaper and magazine articles and concluded, "From billboard advertising to the evening news, from movies to songs on the radio, we are, now more than ever before, confronted by the media at all turns. What was to be a marketplace of ideas, has been reduced to simply a marketplace that has replaced democratic ideals with bottom lines."

Listen in college classrooms, dinner-table conversations, or intimate marital dialogue and you will hear that accountants' term applied to all areas of life. Indeed, the "bottom line" symbolizes contemporary cultural values. Advertisers attempt to convince each "consumer" that he or she is and should be the focus of attention and as such can overcome the severe inadequacies from which he or she suffers by buying something, at the mall or online.

When tragedies strike the nation, like the 9/11 attacks, George W. Bush, the religious president, recommends shopping as a spiritual placebo, as if God had programmed Adam and Eve with genes that would gradually evolve into full-blown shopping compulsions. By developing the shopping habit, one can spend (pun intended) one's days in a truly meaningful activity (strong hints abound in the more affluent communities that there is no necessary time limit on lifespan if you buy the proper ingredients to renew your organs, skin, bone, and muscle and find the proper surgeons who can replace worn-out parts). If the "system" refers to anything in the early twenty-first century, it is the unchallenged acceptance of a triangulated process of production–advertising–consumption as the best, and only, of all possible cultures. And don't forget to pray in your spare time, so God will bless you with more money to shop. Or, if He doesn't, you must have done something unforgivable.

Shopping might constitute the one shared American value in the twenty-first century. Certainly not voting! We disagree as a people about the certainty and proximity of Armageddon and the imminence of the Kingdom of the Apocalypse, on the right (or wrong) to have abortions, and the inherent virtue of gun ownership. But "malling," "Ebaying," and "amazon-dot-com-ing" have become as American as the proverbial apple pie.

Periodically, as in the 1960s, the children of the educated rebel against "the system." The hypocrisy of promoting democracy abroad while denying it to people of color at home, for example, helped motivate the entry of thousands of young whites, and blacks, into the civil rights movement. In his dramatic 1964 Berkeley Free Speech Movement address at Sproul Plaza, Mario Savio, who spent time in Mississippi as a civil rights worker, defined the cultural revolt when he voiced the concern over students, all human beings, being "reduced to punch cards that shouldn't be spindled and mutilated." Savio, who stuttered when in conversation, developed a vibrant style of oratory. Some of his professors thought about how this young moralist had found cultural links to Walt Whitman as he declared himself and his fellow students to stand for the American culture that valued the individual, not individualism.

Savio and many of those who joined that larger "movement" believed that the culture had miscast people as "consumers." These young people demanded recognition as actors in their own history rather than as obedient parasites, conditioned to take things from the world in order to correct various "personal" inadequacies.

If shopping doesn't distract the aspiring historical actor, the very rules and regulations of the national security state form a veritable obstacle course to participation. National security culture assumes that government officials should "classify" millions of documents each month as a simple routine function of imperial democracy in the twenty-first century, thus making government unaccountable. Beyond voting—which most Americans don't engage in—the political system does little to encourage meaningful citizen participation.

When national security as the dominant strain in official political culture marries shopping as the most encouraged spiritual activity, it should not surprise anyone that the country experiences a revival of fundamentalist religion. During the week, the consumer should not question but shop "till you drop;" on Sunday, Rev. Jerry Falwell and company will scare you sinners with the Devil waiting to capture your soul. On the other hand, Rapture calls, if only Israel can continue her wars and bring on Armageddon.

Such ideological pap serves well the multinational corporations, the prime beneficiaries of addictive shopping and national security secrecy. Wal-Mart sucked in bargain-hunting shoppers and McDonnell-Douglas scored multibillion dollar contracts for worthless weapons systems. So prestigious had Sam Walton's business model become (pay minimum wage, don't permit unions, and exploit your workers to the max) that leading business schools have begun to teach his methods. Some of these epigones of business culture attend church regularly and religiously support the Republican Party. For all of their alleged piety, leading corporate executives seem to have no compunctions about straying beyond the windy side of the law. As twenty-first century scandals have already revealed, some of the largest and best politically connected companies stole billions from the public. Thus far, most of their CEOs have escaped serious punishment.

The myth of corporate culture, "the more private, the better," continues to pervade the media and the universities. Since the onset of the Reagan Administration in 1981, the official word has come down: government is bad; don't pay taxes to it; the private sector is good; use it to replace government.

In 2003, government collapsed in many parts of the United States. Schools closed five weeks early in Oregon. State and local prisons and jails had to release prisoners. Police could not put dangerous felons behind bars. No money! California suffered a $38 billion and still-rising deficit, some of it brought on by the billions of dollars stolen from it by the energy swindle perpetrated by Enron during the 2001 energy crisis.

The icons of business culture, such as former Enron CEO Kenneth Lay, who had bribed (contributed to the campaigns of) the models of political culture, proved themselves no better than a gang of thieves. The hot air escaped from the balloon that carried the mystique of corporate culture. The Enron and WorldCom CEOs who posed as efficient managers proved themselves no better than high-level scam artists.

The culture that merged shopping, fundamentalist religion, and corporate virtue proved not only outrageously thin and irrational, but downright destructive. It tried and still succeeds with millions of Americans in disassociating people from their interests.

It will require struggle to bring culture out of its corrupted Petri dish of contemporary national security–mass consumption disguised as "individualism" and onto the high road of decency. Those who lived through the 1960s as participants in the movement for change can assure younger generations of how much fun they had engaging in politics and culture, not just as spectators. In those days, notions of citizenship had not yet faded from their proper place in the epistemological mold.

Lest nostalgia for the old ways and days drip onto the pages of books and periodicals from the pens of aging hippies and leftist agitators, look closely at how the other side has gained the cultural and political high ground. Those whom we once dismissed as the prim and prissy right wing (the John Ashcrofts and Tom DeLays), along with the neocon contingent (like Richard Perle and Paul Wolfowitz), disparage the '60s as immoral, undisciplined, and at times unpatriotic.

The political and cultural wars of the 1960s between the politics of empire and consumption on the one hand and the return to the values of republicanism and citizenship (participation) continue. In the early twenty-first century, the children and grandchildren of the '60s generation, the young and old protestors, engaged against the undemocratic WTO in Seattle or demonstrated against imperialism as Bush marched inextricably toward war with Iraq. The generation that protested against the limiting of free speech in the 1960s in the cold war against communism has given ideological birth to those who now protest against limits placed on civil liberties under the USA Patriot Act in the name of "fighting" terrorism. But underneath the political issues lies the core of culture, that essence of social interaction that gets passed on when political and economic systems decay.

We all face the material world in which under advanced capitalism technology changes our lives with lightning speed, because faster means better. It alters our sense of time and space ("damn, it's taken over three seconds to get online"), dictates life patterns, transportation modes, and notions of how we confront "reality."

It has also become apparent that the dynamics that define modern culture, the movements of capital, and the accelerated growth of technology have systematically uprooted "traditional" cultures. They have all but destroyed what Marx called "rural idiocy" or "idyllic feudalism," which includes remnants of slavery and involuntary servitude throughout the "underdeveloped" world and in the homes of some well-paid officials of the IMF and World Bank.[2] The impulses of capital in the hands of "investors" have also disturbed healthy if not downright organic relationships that indigenous peoples had developed over centuries with the rest of Nature.

Rebellions against the advancing shopping-center way of being have led to bloody street fighting in certain cities. Substantial publics have formed solidarity links with rebels in the third world who struggle to maintain those values still recognized widely as inherently virtuous. How ironic that the 1994 Mayan uprising in Chiapas reverberated among middle-class people in the United States and Europe; more logically, the Zapatistas[3] attracted strong support from Kurds, Tibetans, indigenous African people, and many who still inhabit "reserves" and "reservations" in the Western Hemisphere.

On college campuses, such movements have succeeded in involving the most sensitive students and faculty members. Currently, a surprising number of students have also become committed to the justice movement for low-wage, mostly foreign-born workers. Students, who for the decades of the 1980s and 1990s appeared passive and docile, unquestioningly accepting the credit-card culture as both good and necessary, have now begun to protest sweatshop conditions, demonstrate for underpaid janitors, and forge solidarity with the indigenous people of Chiapas. Where will these movements go? They share a set of values, cultural and political, that would undermine the shopping mandate.

The American man (women can watch also) has special license to

watch one or another fabulous production of what is loosely called
"sports." Watching, a vicarious experience, has replaced all meaningful
forms of action in the acceptable popular culture. TV, after all, commands each person: Watch me—or you might miss something that could
point out another of your potentially correctable inadequacies. Once
involved in political activities, students watch less TV, and spend less
time in flirty chat rooms and vertigo-producing department stores. This
behavior alone makes them outcasts from the "cool" world, if not downright unpatriotic. Thus far, the mass marketers have not figured out how
to transform the attributes of the new student movements into commodities as they did during the cultural rebellion of the 1960s. This new
generation understands digital technology and after spending a day organizing, uses it to enjoy listening to Beethoven, rather than hearing his
"Ode to Joy" used as background music for a car commercial or cell
phone ring.

A multiculture linking indigenous people to poor working people
through traditional ideals of justice and equality becomes inherently subversive. This combined and diverse culture of decency in any
language, the high road of our collective past, could serve as a stimulus to find what Americans have long sought: freedom, in all of its
highest forms. As José Marti phrased it: to be cultured is to be free.

Freedom to absorb the high culture of art, literature, music, sports,
science, and political philosophy requires freedom from the dictates
of shopping. It means constructing from the many beautiful and often
discarded parts of our past an alternative culture, one that Americans
once referred to as the source of traditional values. The Puritan writers
tried to focus the flock's attention on spiritual salvation, hardly a consumerist notion. The nineteenth- and even some early twentieth-century
poets and novelists filled their works with notions of salvation, pitting
man against and with Nature (Hemingway and earlier Melville,
who issued warnings not to attempt to dominate areas where God's will
obviously prevails), the quest for organic relationships (Thoreau), and
serenity through spiritual exercises.

Some of the great philosophers and novelists of the twentieth century
offered ways to seek justice or alternatively the common good, through
class struggle or more dialogic exercises. Much of the rich writing of the
past, however, has fallen into states of disuse; ideas, like a cultural oil
well, bubbling near the surface, await someone to direct publics on how
to use their collective mind so as to focus intellectual energy toward

meaningful activity. By reaching back into this treasure chest the citizen can regain his identity and strip away the imposed Saran Wrap overlay of consumerism. The commercial psyche, replete with mindless anxieties, conditions people to turn away from their human quality, from their inherently social nature. So, we had better separate our identities from the commercial packaging and rediscover that link to the art and beauty that resides in our past in all of us.

1

The Bush Vision
A Bipolar Political Disorder

It is clear our nation is reliant upon big foreign oil.
More and more of our imports come from overseas.
—G.W. Bush, Beaverton, OR,
September 25, 2000

The Culture of Naked Power

I assumed that the head of a large empire possesses a world vision, some sense that his policies coincide with a linguistic roadmap that goes beyond phrases such as "they hate us," "bring 'em on," and "we love freedom." One could become frustrated, however, trying to find connections between President Bush's post-9/11 words and the big issues, such as the future of the environment or the fate of more than half the world's desperately poor people.

Since the Supreme Court selected him before the vote-counters in Florida could complete their task, W's behavior has certainly evolved. From a crude and simplistic view of the world as Texas Governor, he has built on his old prejudices and added new twists in his mutation as official imperial manager.

A long-time Washington observer confided that thanks to Bush he finally understood long-term US imperial strategy, "We're bigger and stronger than the rest of you varmints and if you step out of line we'll kick your ass."

Similarly, in his approach to domestic politics, Bush shows scant respect for the rule of law. Crime, on the other hand, has always played a crucial role in W's Texas-Yale *weltanschauung*. Years before invading Iraq, as Texas Governor, Bush emphasized that wrongdoers merited harsh punishment. Rehabilitating criminals sounded like advice from bleeding heart liberals. Later on, those same softies urged him to let the UN weapons inspectors do their job in Iraq. No matter. "Saddam refused to let them in," he said. Well, that's how he remembered it. Hard to keep track of so many facts when you're running a country! Leaders must trust their instincts and guide those feelings with religious compassion. That's what he learned, or memorized.

But the Governor refused to extend his "compassionate conservatism" to those evil people on death row. In his five years as governor he presided over 152 executions, more than any other state leader. And they all deserved it. "Every person that has been put to death in Texas under my watch has been guilty of the crime charged, and has had full access to the courts," he declared in February 2001. A leader cannot afford to vacillate. He must stand behind his decisions and not be swayed by intellectual argument.

Indeed, as Anthony Lewis "argued" in his June 17, 2000 *New York Times* column, one-third of those executed under Bush had trial or appeal lawyers who were later disbarred or otherwise sanctioned. In forty cases the lawyers presented no evidence at all or only one witness at the sentencing phase of the trial. In almost thirty other cases, prosecutors used psychiatric testimony based on experts who had not even interviewed the people on trial.

Bush dismissed both doubts and doubters. "We've adequately answered innocence or guilt," Bush smugly responded to an Associated Press reporter in an article titled "Texas Death Row-Cases Questioned," June 11, 2000. Every defendant, he claimed "had full access to a fair trial." Bush seems to need certainty so badly that he simply cannot deal with evidence that might refute his position.

As president, Bush has apparently reconsidered his stance on criminals, well, certain kinds anyway. His executive rehabilitation program calls for the appointment to high policy posts of former felons who have links to mass murder, not just simple homicide. These lawbreakers had also shown their utter contempt for the lives of Central Americans, the US Congress, and the Constitution as well.

Take as examples officials he named to manage important policy positions: Elliot Abrams, appointed to the National Security Council; John Poindexter, head of the Information Awareness Office; John Negroponte, the Permanent US Representative to the United Nations; and Otto Reich, a Latin America envoy.

These four characters conspired to circumvent Congress in the 1980s. Because the CIA-backed Contras had committed human rights violations and blatant acts of terrorism, Congress defunded them in 1985. In 1981, President Reagan had chosen the universally discredited Contras to depose the leftist government of Nicaragua. The kill-crazy Contras, however, had acquired serious admirers in Washington, including the four above-mentioned characters. These high-placed conspirators decided to sell missiles to Iran (also prohibited by Congress) so that they could funnel the proceeds to their beloved Contras, and then cover it up.

In his testimony to Congress, the scrappy Abrams made witness history when he declared, "I never said I had no idea about most of the things you said I had no idea about." Abrams also explained in his autobiography that he had to inform his young children about the headline announcing his indictment, so he told them he had to lie to Congress to protect the national interest.

The then Deputy Assistant Secretary of State to Central America pleaded guilty to withholding information from Congress and received two years probation and one hundred hours community work. Now, the "pardoned" Abrams as the new White House man on the Middle East, having learned that one can get away with felonious behavior if one maintains close links to the Bush family, will attempt to redraw the roadmap of the Middle East. Secretary of State Colin Powell drafted a plan for designing a peaceful solution and eventually a Palestinian state. The vision, by deduction, amounts to a virtual rubber stamp for Israeli repression and continued expansion into Palestinian territory. It also coincides with Abrams' stated belief that Israel and the United States will benefit from tighter connections with the far-right fundamentalist Christians who want Israel to prevail and occupy all of Palestine and US policy.

Retired Admiral and former National Security Adviser to Reagan, John Poindexter was convicted of five felonies involving conspiracy, obstruction of Congress, and making false statements. The judge gave him six months in prison, but an appellate court reversed the sentence because Congress had previously granted him immunity. His slipping out of prison on a procedural error does not change the facts of the case. Poindexter's vision runs toward secrecy and circumventing law. In his latest declaration, he assures the public that the privacy of individuals will not be affected by his snooping into their private affairs as he looks for terrorists. (In August 2003, Poindexter announced his resignation as the head of the Pentagon's Defense Advanced Research Project Agency, after Congress learned that his office had bankrolled a now-cancelled stock-market-like Web site designed to help policy makers predict future terrorist activities.)[1]

Otto Reich ran Latin America policy until November 2002 and now holds a special appointment from the White House for Latin America. Critics called Reich the Minister of Lying, an appropriate title for his previous post as Reagan's head of the Office of Public Diplomacy and less than artful coverups of human rights violations by the Contras.

Negroponte, now Ambassador to the United Nations, also played the Iran-Contra game, covering up human rights abuses by "our" military friends in Honduras and narrowly escaping indictment. What liberal critics called human rights abuse, Reich and Negroponte understood as necessary for US national security, that you can't make an omelet without breaking the eggs, or some such Maoism.

By appointing these characters, W's worldview (apologies to philosophers) becomes clearer. Those who participated in criminal plots that caused the deaths of tens of thousands in Central America will have a second chance to show the public what they really stand for. Indeed, they remain as role models for the United States in its post-republican incarnation.

Neither Congress nor the media chose to focus on those appointments. Indeed, part of the mass media grew downright imperial and hired some former Iran-Contra felons as commentators. Lt. Col. Oliver North worked for CNN and Fox. Other convicted felons, such as G. Gordon Liddy of Watergate notoriety, host their own radio shows. Fox News and other Rupert Murdoch outlets, along with ABC Radio and Clear Channel's 1200 radio stations, flagrantly push the Bush agenda and encourage their talk-show hosts to insult as unpatriotic those who disagreed with making war on Iraq. Sean Hannity and Larry Elder, Rush Limbaugh and Al Rantel shout and scream at those who take issue with Bush's policies.

This aggressive war game played over the media diverts that sector of the public that is not involved with the trivialities of everyday sex and "reality" television.

Naturally, when the White House released its National Security Plan in September 2002 the nattering right-wing talk-show hosts didn't mention that in its quest for "full spectral dominance," it further shredded the republican fabric. In the plan, the Bill of Rights took a distant second place.

What role will Congress play in this new imperial obsession? Past notions of accountability and openness, when administrations felt it necessary to at least try to cover imperial expeditions with vestiges of republican organs, have slipped into disuse. After 9/11, most members feared that they would find themselves labeled "unpatriotic" if they dissented on issues involving granting the president expanded war-making powers and restricting liberties. And instead of voting their conscience, many voted their convenience.

We have seen no evidence that the president has given any of these institution-changing notions the slightest bit of thought or reflection. Bush listens to his trusted advisers, led by the Svengali-like Karl Rove, and promotes unashamedly the notions that America stands for freedom and justice under God. "God Bless America," he says repeatedly, and the American way of life, one shared more or less by majorities in Western Europe, Japan, Australia, and New Zealand.

For W, the good life, the one God intended, means that leisure, pleasure, and relaxation, based on the individual's freedom to buy commodities, will presumably satisfy any and all reasonable human urges. Implicit in this paradigm is God's reward for the wealthy in the United States, who should play all the real or video golf they want and pay no taxes. God holds out a promise for the rest of the world: they too can succeed by adopting the American set of values.

The US government under this image exercises naked imperial power to bring noncompliant nations into the global corporate model under the guise of saving the world from Islamic terrorists and drug traffickers, making everything more democratic and, of course, protecting our interests, which are usually "classified."

The few dissenters to this overarching scheme demand changes in Middle East policy that reflect regional realities and notions of equality and justice. They feel, correctly, vulnerable to attacks on their patriotism. Those who focus on the immediate needs of the impoverished three-billion-plus people, and the screaming demands of the environment, where the ice-melting phenomenon has scientists truly concerned, just don't understand the culture of power.

In Bush's mind, power derives from the assumption that God has placed Nature in man's path for his immediate and perpetual use. Trees are for chopping down, and then for packing crates, toothpicks, paper, and furniture, of course; animals are to kill for meat, hide, and sport; fish to catch; land to develop and drill on, and so on. Those who refer to income gaps incite "class warfare." However mad it may seem, this vision symbolizes the "nature" of the people who currently manipulate power and wealth, and Nature.

Bush relates best to men who exercise power without thought of consequences, like Israeli Prime Minister Ariel Sharon, whom he called "a man of peace," and members of the Saudi royal family, some of whom he hosted at his ranch. Sharon's vision of a greater Israel coincides with Bush's theological supporters, like the Reverends Jerry Falwell and Pat Robertson, whose biblical mumbo-jumbo demands that Israel conquer the Middle East. The oily Saudis, who ooze piety and affluence, literally fuel the imperial drive.

The logic of naked imperial power also includes a world of bizarre contrasts. As Wade Davis underlines in the July 6, 2002 *Globe & Mail*, Americans spend as much on lawn maintenance as the government of India collects in federal tax revenue.

The Bush vision of a world under the thumb of US power requires a $400 billion defense budget, larger than the entire economy of Australia. Yet, more than one-sixth of the world's population exists on less than one dollar a day.

Bush grew up with commercial values, and alcohol, and knows only one notion of development. He seems unable to understand that his model has failed in the Middle East and throughout the third world. Those third-world leaders who accepted "business wisdom" as expressed in the IMF and World Bank development models have led their economies to disaster, bankrupt Argentina is a recent dramatic example.

Indeed, the IMF model assumes high consumption of energy and destruction of resources. It has led to serious environmental damage. It may coincide with business logic, but does not coincide with the realities of Nature. It has put Bush's economic policies and the facts of earth on a collision course.

Bush assumes that science and technology, the cause of some of the acute problems, can solve whatever issues arise. Look how many babies now live that once would have perished. The whole world enjoys increased life expectancy, but if one looks deeper into the kind of lives that third-world people lead, one sees something that obviously escapes George W's vision. An Asian garment worker sewing jeans for The Gap makes about $88 a month, much less than the hourly salary of many US CEOs, professionals, athletes, and entertainers. That is, he literally falls into the gap, as The Gap's advertisement inadvertently tells us.

The majority of the world will not share in Bush's world. Nor does he envision them participating. Bush's vision presumes that the majority of the world's people can and will forget the past, culture, values, and language, and become one with the commodity culture, the only one he can imagine, and from which his vision of power has emerged. That power rests on immense wealth, including his family's, his Republican supporters, and military potency.

What the once innocent Americans have learned through 9/11, however, is that neither their government's wealth nor military power translates into security. America can continue to export stale *Baywatch* episodes into remote hamlets throughout the Middle East, but that will not stop the melting of polar ice caps, the warming of the globe, or the rising of the ocean levels, nor will it touch the scourge of poverty.

The Bush world view includes not just the exporting of old *Dallas* reruns and T&A shows, but refer also to the exercise of naked imperial power in the Middle East.

Ironically, only criminal methods can realize W's world vision.[2] His culture of power means a government of men, not laws, willing to subjugate, dominate, and impose their will on people and nature.

If you agree with this analysis then you'll conclude, as I have, that we face a dangerous situation and you will thus be motivated to get off your ass and do something about it.

Revised: August 2003

Politics and the Enron Scandal, Part I:
The Enron System Works—
Well, for Some People!

> I would love to personally escort Lay to an 8-by-10 cell that he
> could share with a tattooed dude who says, 'Hi, my name is
> Spike, honey.'
> —California Attorney General Bill Lockyer,
> the *Wall Street Journal*, May 2001

My liberal friends insist that the 2001 Enron disaster proves that the
system doesn't work. Never has such a giant corporation gone belly-up.
$60 billion of shareholder investment evaporated along with an esti-
mated $1.3 billion in the retirement accounts of Enron workers.

Enron's collapse and similar implosions at WorldCom and Adelphia,
demonstrate both the nature of capitalism's value system at its highest
levels of greed, corruption, and thievery, as well as the power of corporate money to block government agencies from protecting the public.

In November 2001, Enron reported that it had overstated its net
income dating back to 1997 by $586 million. That confession led to the
proverbial snowball descending the mountain, culminating in Enron's
bankruptcy. The SEC failed to stop the accounting company, Arthur
Andersen, from doing consulting work for the very company they were
auditing.

In 2001, the Arthur Andersen accounting firm made a $52 million fee
for servicing Enron. So, the business executives planned the scam, the
accountants abetted it through bookkeeping, and the bankers knowingly
financed the fraud.[3] Together, this criminal triad concealed billions in
debts so that they didn't reflect negatively on the company's balance
sheets.

Enron traded energy like hog bellies and grew in fifteen years into the
seventh largest American company. Enron employed some 21,000 people
in over forty countries. But the firm's lightning rise to business stardom
by "trading" something that didn't need "trading" turned to swindle, as
a kind of logical business practice.

The supposedly infallible regulatory agencies allowed this massive hanky-panky to go forward. As a result, Enron executives deprived thousands of people of their pension plans, and manipulated the California energy market, gulling residents of that state out of billions. For the time being, the shockwave stopped the energy lobbyists' chatter about deregulating all corporate activities. The question arises from the Enron debacle: exactly what system does or doesn't work, and for whom?

For example, the system worked well for Texas Governor Rick Perry (R), who received from Enron more than $200,000 from 1997 through July 2001. Perry used the money to build his campaign war chest and ate some sumptuous free meals to boot. But when his Democratic gubernatorial challengers said that ethics demand that he donate the tainted money to a fund for laid-off Enron workers, he belched and told his foes to go stuff it.

He had worked within the "system" in the heart of Texas, USA. The thousands who lost their Enron jobs and the tens of thousands who watched their retirement savings disappear when the company's stock crashed now understand the nature of the system. It works for Governor Perry, but not so well for them. Who said that our great free enterprise system, which has secured the fortunes of the wealthy classes through depression and boom, through war (especially), and even peace ought also to provide security for the less wealthy? Did anyone learn that lesson in school? Certainly not in private school! Who said that "works" included everyone?

Enron executives understood that the system offered ways to make lots of money if you could convince (buy) politicians to change some laws and persuade (bribe) administrators to rule in your favor. That, by the way, is exactly how the system works.

So, the Enron bosses, freed from regulation and careful scrutiny by the system's own rules, organized a network of some two thousand subsidiaries in more than twenty states and sixty foreign countries. Enron established subsidiaries in offshore tax havens such as the Cayman Islands; others they set up under legal loopholes in Brazil and England.

But to hide their business (gambling?) losses and then have the stockholders (pensioners) pay the sordid debts of phantom companies they had hidden from public view, Enron executives didn't use only overseas arrangements.

They had also made Delaware the home to the 685 Enron subsidiaries. Enron's accounting shenanigans worked in Delaware. So, the system worked, for the lawyers and other intermediaries whose employment is derived from the creation and sustenance of corporate accounting tricks.

An Enron exec didn't even have to go to Delaware to start a corporate entity in, say, Wilmington, the state's largest city. Just surf the Web or scan a business magazine in the dentist's waiting room and you'll see ads for Delaware-registered corporation agents. For less than $100 you can open a business in a place where you've never been, without an office, phone number, or any personnel. It's magic. You don't have to tell anyone how much you're making or losing, or what business you're actually doing. Supposedly, these Delaware entities had invested in foreign power plants. In fact, you can register your corporation under the name of Alfred E. Newman and literally not have to worry that anyone will get suspicious or even care. What a system! Enron's chartered subsidiaries in Delaware lost more than $400 million from the late 1990s on.

Delaware offers corporate hustlers speed, secrecy, and state tax exemptions. The state also woos slimy corporate customers by advertising its business-friendly courts. Thanks to this wholesome atmosphere, you can find the stolid old conservative Fortune 500 alongside international criminals. They all share a common interest in laundering money, so as not to pay taxes, to hide losses or gains from stockholders and regulators, and in general to screw someone in the course of making money.

That defines the system. And, boy does it work—for those who have the funds to hire the best lawyers and accountants to do the paperwork. The system actually encourages wealthy scoundrels to circumvent taxes and elementary accountability; the rascals' lawyers and accountants have learned the system in our top business and law schools so that after they get their MBAs and law degrees they can help slide their slimy clients through the laws' narrowest loopholes.

But so greedy had the Enron executives become, that even their own accountants blew warning bugles. So, the duplicitous executives began to dump their Enron stock as it started its downward spiral, while simultaneously urging employees and pensioners to buy the very stock they knew had serious problems. Worse, while CEOs sold literally millions of their own shares they concurrently forbade company employees from selling any of their Enron stock. The system, they said, didn't disallow such a practice.

The system also allowed for "accounting errors" of $1 billion in "equity adjustments" from another Delaware partnership. Delaware has chartered more than half a million businesses that can practice voodoo accounting and still remain on the windy side of the law.

The system also works to link politics to wealth in the most direct way. Aside from getting uncountable favors and connections from government and elected officials, such as passing deregulatory laws for energy sales and commerce, Enron also managed to place its people in decision-making posts at many levels of government.

In Texas, Governor Perry named former Enron executive Max Yzaguirre to head the powerful Public Utilities Commission. In typical subtle Enron style, Kenneth Lay, Enron's top dog, donated $25,000 to Perry. "It's totally coincidental," Mr. Perry declared in December of last year. Such "coincidences" help the system to work, of course.

Also coincidentally, Enron contributed heavily to California Governor Gray Davis' campaign and California under Davis bought energy from Enron at inflated prices when the state ran short in the summer of 2001. Another systemic coincidence!

The most interesting of all the Enron forays into public policy took them to the vice president's office. Aside from his own stock interest, Dick Cheney saw the Enron Corporation as the essence of the system he loved. So, he called upon Enron execs, appointed to his energy task force, to formulate the national energy plan, the discussion of which he now claims was "private."

What a wonderful sense of propriety Cheney possesses. He couldn't wait to make public the details of Bill Clinton's White House gropings of Monica, but when it comes to a policy of importance to all Americans, he invokes his privacy protections. He has yet to reveal the nature of the conversations he had with these high-salaried shoplifters. That's how Cheney's system works.

The system has also worked for the media. Stories like the Enron scandal furnish them with the kind of ammunition their bosses love: the press has broken down the outrage into shotgun pellets of information and fires them daily at the public. The stories don't seem to cohere; just another corporate scandal, too complicated for us nonexperts to comprehend.

The personalities behind the scandal and their families appear as "news" that the average citizen can understand. A woman who works with me sympathized with former Enron chief exec, "poor Ken Lay." She shook her head and told me that "I saw his wife weep on that NBC interview and I felt for her and her family," referring to Linda Lay's January 28, 2002 interview on NBC's *Today* show.

"Yes, poor Ken Lay," I thought to myself, "a man worth billions and now down to his last $100 million!" Worse, the president of the United States, the man who nicknamed him "Kenny Boy," has now distanced himself from his former benefactor and calls him "Mr. Lay." Imagine Kenny Boy's hurt feelings!

Note that NBC did not interview any of the tens of thousands of poor and middle-class people who lost their pensions while Ken Lay sold his stock for hundreds of millions, supposedly to pay debts on another of his business-gambling enterprises. Sure, focus on the filthy rich who have lost part of their fortunes, not on the poor who have lost their jobs and pensions. The poor, presumably, are not worth media attention because they don't possess large enough fortunes.

One positive outcome of the scandal is that we now hear less talk of "privatizing social security." Suppose the Bushies had won that battle! Even more people would have had their retirement accounts in Enron stocks! See, the system works!

The Enron execs won't run into the California Three Strikes Law[4] assuming they go to trial and get convicted. But the sensationalizing media adore stories about rich people getting into trouble. They're just like the rest of us, F. Scott Fitzgerald remarked, except they have more money. He also observed in *The Great Gatsby* that the rich make messes and expect others to clean up after them. And they take money more seriously than poor people do.

In the late 1970s, I read an obit in the *New York Times*, citing the strange case of Eli Black, former CEO of United Brands (Fruit). Black had committed suicide after suffering a series of business reversals. Nevertheless, experts estimated the value of his estate at some $60 million. "Why," I asked a business friend, "would a man with that kind of wealth kill himself?"

My rich friend looked at me as if I understood nothing. "If he had lived," he replied, "he stood to lose millions more."

Should we put a suicide watch on Ken Lay and the other former Enron execs who stand to lose millions more? Are the decline of his fortune and his wife's tears evidence of the system working? Or have a small gang of thieves, disguised as business executives in collusion with government officials, pulled a major fast one on the public?

Notice that Ashcroft, Cheney, and Bush have not suggested that any of the thieves who bilked the public for billions should be sent to Camp X-ray in Guantánamo! Indeed, these people have behaved like traitors and economic terrorists.

Let's hope that the core of their criminal activities doesn't get lost in the media and congressional circuses that have just opened and will soon close. Enron is about a system, not an aberration. This system screwed hundreds of thousands and worked very well for a small group of very sleazy people—right on up to the White House.

January 2002

Enron, Part II:
Sex and the Enron Scam

My daughter asked whether I saw similarities between Bill Clinton's White House sex scandal and the unfolding Enron ignominy.

I shrugged my shoulders, unable to make such a comparison. Remember when Bill Clinton said, "I didn't have sex with that woman" and then he went on to engage in a semantic dispute about the meaning of the word "sex?" In fact, Monica agreed with him that what they did together wasn't sex, but just playing around.

"But most of us didn't think that Clinton and Monica's, how shall I say it, fine distinction altered the basic fact. But how does this relate to Enron's hanky-panky with George W. Bush?"

"Bush told us earlier this month that he 'hardly' knew Kenny Boy, I mean 'Mister Lay,'" she insisted. "You see, he might be doing with the word 'hardly' what Bill Clinton did with 'sex.'"

"Well," I advised her, "don't wait for a semantic debate on the word 'hardly.'"

"Both Monica Lewinsky and Ken Lay occupied places in the White House where they didn't belong. Monica tempted the ever-horny Clinton with her cleavage and Kenny Boy tempted W—and his father—with money. Monica never spent the night as Kenny Boy did, and she wasn't as careful about cleaning up the evidence."

"Huh?" I said.

"Monica didn't even take her telltale stained dress to the cleaners while Kenny Boy had his minions shred thousands of incriminating documents."

"Ah," I said. "I think I see where you're going with this."

"Kenny Boy might not have had the kind of intimate contact with W that Monica had with Bill, but he sure has stained the reputation of the ruling family and many others as well. Monica might have wanted a low- or mid-level job at the White House for her labors, but Kenny Boy wanted and got billions of dollars in profits for his close relationship with power. Thanks to his intimacy with high officials, an intimacy gained through a straight money transaction—isn't that called prostitution by the way?—Kenny Boy got laws written for Enron's benefit, he got regulatory agencies to stop regulating, and he even got Vice President Dick Cheney to use Enron executives as his key consultants for an energy plan. My God, Enron may even have influenced Bush's decision not to sign the Kyoto environment accords."

"Wow," I said. "You're really creative."

"Thanks," she said. "But I have this report to my rhetoric class and I'm trying to make the case that a president telling lies about his intimate relations with top corporate executives might transcend as political evil lying about sex in the White House. What do you think?"

January 2002

Some months and several scandalous events later, we resumed the discussion.

A Dialogue about
Sex, Violence, and the Budget

I try to explain US politics to my teenager as we sit together and absorb distracting TV sound-bites. "The budget," I explain patiently, "provides the key to understanding the core of our system. After all, in the budget decisions," I continue, "we see how the national pie gets cut, who gets the big pieces, and who must settle for the crumbs."

She shakes her head in disbelief as the riveting local evening news unfolds.

"Images of sex and violence," I explain as she watches reports of murder, rape, and arson, "tend to obscure your view of the budget."

She sneers at me.

"Listen," I admit, "sex stories have their place in the news."

"Viva Bill and Monica," she retorts.

"And," I continue, "violence in places like the Middle East and Kashmir belongs in the news. But," I argue, "rarely will the media provide a proper context for its sexy and violent stories. That is, the media doesn't tell us from where the daily violence arises, what a Southern California couple's mate-swapping behavior had to do with the murder of their child. So, without explanation," I conclude, "we the public feel the distracting flashes of thrill and danger rather than the dull pounding of class analysis."

She was listening to the TV reporter describing the gory details about a fire in a housing complex. Then the anchor turned his attention to Washington. "DC police discovered in Rock Creek Park the murdered remains of Chandra Levy, the missing congressional intern."

"I read just a few weeks ago," she said, "in a supermarket tabloid that some clairvoyant suspected that Chandra might have eloped with Osama bin Laden to some Muslim-Jewish Shangri-La."

"Ha," I replied, "that's exactly what I mean. While police searched for Chandra, the media had a field day, but buried the political story about members of Congress debating on how to reward the wealthiest and best-connected—to power—corporations."

"But," she argued, "Chandra being missing was a hot story because she had been involved with a Congressman who some thought might even have murdered her."

"Yes," I said, "the media spent considerable time and little thought on this story at the expense of the parents of this poor woman because she had an affair with Representative Gary Condit. But we learned about Condit the intern-exploiter, not Condit who votes for corporate welfare, the most important fact about this sleazy, Type-A Democrat from Modesto, California. Indeed," I argued, "Condit is the kind of Democrat who has helped remove politics from politics. He has voted for the rich and done little over his years in the House to help the often below-minimum-wage migrant workers who provide us with our food."

"But," she added, "the fact that he hit on interns made the news."

"Exactly," I said. "The media has also spent much time on the search for the tall bearded Muslim fanatic with bad kidneys. After all, W himself said 'we're gonna smoke 'em out.' The media, you see, doesn't distinguish between central and peripheral news in its headlines or bleeding lead stories. A missing intern or a sex scandal outweighs what some old-fashioned conservatives still consider the permanent core of politics: the budget.

"How many viewers, listeners, or readers would stay tuned in to a discussion about the adage, 'What's good for General Motors is good for America?' More important, how many would stay focused on a story that laid out the connections between who wins elections and the amount of tax dollars that went to other large multinational corporations and some smaller ones connected to the current rulers?"

She shrugged.

"For example, we have not seen many clear reports on how the 2001 stimulus bill, which Bush and Congress seemed to have tailored for the benefit of multinational giants, also repealed the alternative minimum tax. I asked two political science professors if they knew about this and they said, 'Huh?' "

"You're lecturing me," she said, as the TV news reported on how firemen had rescued a cute dog that had somehow gotten itself trapped. A little girl was thanking the smiling public officials. "How is anyone supposed to find out the important things?" she asked.

"Well, take a look at groups like the Washington, DC Citizens for Tax Justice. They reported last year that General Motors received $800 million from the repeal of this tax. This Citizens group also revealed that less famous companies linked to Dick Cheney also got big checks. Dallas Power and Light (now called TXU), a company less than five percent the size of GM, got a $600 million check. Less surprising is that Texas-based energy companies like Chevron, Enron, and Phillips Petroleum linked to the Cheney and Bush families received large benefits as well.

"Hey, did you learn in class that those receiving large subsidies under Cheney's energy plan and Congress' stimulus plan also gave monster-sized contributions to the Republican Party?"

She yawned. The smiling weather man had replaced the smiling anchors. He talked about some "good weekend weather" ahead, but didn't mention the causes for the high level of pollution in the Los Angeles air.

"Don't corporations need tax breaks to keep employment high?" she asked me.

"That's part of the myth they've created," I explained. "You see, truly needy companies like IBM, which reported $5.7 billion in US profits last year, also got benefits. Thanks to the repeal of the alternative minimal tax IBM paid less than eleven percent of its pretax US earnings, instead of the thirty-five percent it would have paid if not for the repeal."

"But," she interrupted, "in 2001 President Bush called for a tax cut for everyone. Wasn't that a sign that he cared about poor people?"

"Well," I countered, "it was a sign that he could spin a headline and make a lead story for TV news. But, according to Citizens for Tax Justice, TV news didn't emphasize the hot news, which was that the White House designed its juiciest tax cuts for the richest one percent of all taxpayers. Senate Republicans and a few Democrats went along eagerly."

"So what should the headlines or TV leads have said?" she asked.

"How about: Bush gives $67 to poor; $33,843 to rich."

"You know, Dad, I worry about you," she said. "People who criticize the president like that in these times when we have to stand united could pick up the label of unpatriotic. Our president took the lead in fighting terrorism and explained that we need unity."

"Ha," I retorted, "do you think the road to unity lies in rewarding those who need it least? Do you think that the American people should unite around the theme of giving their hard-earned money to the largest and most bloated corporations, led by the richest people?"

"Those are rhetorical questions," she said.

I ignored her. "The poor who suffered from the 9/11 economic shock-waves didn't receive additional unemployment insurance or health benefits from the president or Congress, just about an average of $67 each in tax cuts. The president apparently thought that his patriotic duty called for rewarding those who needed help least, the very rich."

"Still," she persisted, "Bush tried to keep us calm after 9/11. He suggested that we shop as much as we could and not be afraid to take our families by plane to Disney World. And he says we should donate to the needy."

"You see how the media reports words without explaining them?" I responded. "The president and Congress give away the national treasury to the least deserving and then bleat out messages about Christian charity."

"Chill, Dad," she ordered, seeing that I was working myself up. "Are you accusing Bush of seeking ways to help his richest friends and then intimidating the press corps into behaving like sheep?"

"Hey," I quipped, "if a TV reporter stated that Bush's plan screws the poor, it might not help his journalistic career!"

"Well," she asked, "what was the whole tax break about? We learned in government class that the Democrats took credit for $11 billion in tax rebates in 2001."

"True," I said, "but thirty-five million taxpayers didn't receive much rebate, if anything, because, as Robert McIntyre of Citizens for Tax Justice wrote in October 2001, 'they didn't owe enough in income taxes although they did pay plenty in payroll taxes.'"

She rose during the commercial. "It's hard to figure out how to read budget and tax stories," she said. "I know it's important where our tax money ends up, but how does one focus on it amidst the noise of sex, violence, and shopping?"

"Yes," I replied, "the three Rs of our media educational system. An Osama sighting or a clue about Chandra's murderer will grab media attention, but when the government transfers wealth from our pockets to the wallets of the rich, the media give that little space. 'Family Dies in House Fire' makes front page and lead TV news, but the little-publicized fact that two million New York City residents lack access to healthcare becomes practically a nonstory.

She walked toward the door. "Hey Dad, maybe you could design a system whereby famous people who merit sex and violence headlines could somehow become political educators. They would get our attention and then help us focus on budget allocations. What's Bill Clinton doing these days anyway?"

May 2002

As rumors of Bill Clinton aspiring to run for mayor of New York City grab headlines, the Bushies slowly snuck an old IMF formula into the US budget process. They disguised it as a tax plan, designed to help everyone, of course. But the effect of the "tax cut" marked a major step in the elimination of meaningful government. That is, by reducing the amount in the treasury, while increasing spending on the military, the White House-pushed plan forced Congress to cut social services drastically and block grants to the states. This meant that local and state taxes rose. The poor and middle-class person thus ends up paying more taxes (a few bucks off on federal and a lotta bucks added to state and local) for less services. The result is that the American worker becomes "more productive." Given government's withdrawal of services, she must now pay for what she once took for granted. She thus works harder just to stay afloat. The Bushies disguise this process with rhetoric about big bad government and cutting taxes. They divert some people by focusing on abortion, prayer in school, and the divine right to own a Howitzer. But...

It's the Budget Stupid!— Bush's Lucky Duckies

How does G. W. Bush's ten-year tax plan that purports to return 1.35 trillion dollars to citizens relate to real wealth and real poverty? The very sum itself boggles the mind. I try to imagine what a trillion dollars looks like. And what does it have to do with the price of a bologna sandwich?

For those who deny that poverty still exists in the United States, take a road trip and see it for yourself. You don't have to drive onto Indian reservations to notice the numerous trailer parks nestled on the outskirts of American towns and cities. Most of the residents cannot afford to buy a home or pay rent on an apartment. The rural poor live in ramshackle homes with front yards full of old cars and clotheslines full of tattered garments because they can't afford to pay for a dryer or for the electricity it uses. You see shabbily dressed kids in rural America. In the cities and towns, you don't have to search for ghettoes, barrios, or skid rows. They're ubiquitous.

The poor people, more than 50 million, most without access to health care and free higher education, now lose unemployment insurance. About 800,000 workers got their negative Christmas present when Congress adjourned without renewing their benefits. Another 100,000 a week will exhaust whatever state funds remained according to the Washington DC Center on Budget and Policy Priorities. 2003 will provide devastating challenges to those who got the pink slip in 2002. The official unemployment rate hovers around six percent nationally. Economists expect that figure to increase.

Bush called on Congress to help, but since he has already chosen his military and foreign expenditures and police priorities, it remains unclear where Congress will find funds to help out the unemployed, many of whom might soon become homeless as well.

A December 23, 2002 *USA Today* story uses November data from the Department of Labor that shows long-term unemployment patterns reappearing. "1.7 million workers have been out of work six months or longer—the most since 1994," the story reports. Low-wage workers, usually poorly educated and often from minority groups, generally got their discharge notice first. They are the least able to deal with loss of income and the worst prepared for long-term joblessness.

States typically offer twenty-six weeks of payments, after which workers turn to federal programs that give up to twenty-six more weeks of benefits. But drafters of these programs did not design them to meet the issues of long-term unemployment, which has risen since March 2001.

Along with joblessness, the poor and middle class lose vital services. California Governor Gray Davis announced an almost four-percent cut in education affecting kindergarten through twelfth grade. To make up a $6 million deficit in the prison budget, Kentucky Governor Paul Patton released 567 prisoners prematurely. "It's not going to be pretty," he said.

The compassionate conservative Bush government has thrown the ball where it said it belongs, to the private charities. But the filthy rich, the reputed backbone of philanthropy, have reduced their donations to the poor but not the six-figure or more salaries paid to the CEOs of the charities.

After a decade of relative prosperity, the middle and working classes ran up their credit-card debts. *USA Today* cited *CardWeb.com,* which tracks credit-card trends, to show that the average household had almost $8500 worth of credit-card debt in 2002, an increase of 160 percent in the past decade.[5]

As we know, under compassionate conservatism, the Bush government has slashed the social budget while elevating the military and (while cutting benefits to members of the military) "security" budgets to a record high of $400 billion while simultaneously cutting taxes. The president, with congressional approval, has shifted the burden of maintaining a highly unequal social order to the states, the very entities that failed to meet such a challenge in the early 1930s.

Indeed, the New Deal arose because charity didn't work. The federal government had to take an active and guiding hand in alleviating mass misery, or face possible revolution. Now, the federal government, the entity that commands trillions of dollars, refuses to shell out to the people who most need them, but insists that the way to make the poor more secure is to reward the already rewarded. In turn, the billionaires will invest and jobs will appear—the Bush logic. We'll see.

As if to emphasize the idea of rewarding the least needy, Bush restored cash bonuses to his political appointees, those least needy and least qualified. The irony of this move was not lost on regular government workers whose raises Bush reduced from 4.1 to 3.1 percent, claiming that the war on terrorism had forced this move.

Compassionate conservatism has become the euphemism for "screw the poor and have a good laugh at their expense." Administration insiders and *Wall Street Journal* editors have found a new label for the poorest of Americans. These "lucky duckies," because they don't have to pay much income tax compared to the deeply disadvantaged multibillionaires, have had a free ride for too long. Why not put a federal tax bite into their $6.35-an-hour wages as well as the $10,000 an hour "earned" by those of good breeding? Mark Twain defined good breeding as consisting "of concealing how much we think of ourselves and how little we think of the other person."

The Bush electoral "victory" followed by his high post-9/11 ratings appear to have made possible the dream of the greediest of the disgustingly rich class to amass more, consume more, and make fun of those who have less. Rush Limbaugh, my favorite right-wing radio huckster, gives the process of looting the national treasury an ideological bent. He insists that tax cutting means conservatism. Do not give a penny to the entity that provides schools, roads, sewage, and other necessities. It's all right, however, to have the government subsidize agribusiness directly and other enormous corporate conglomerations indirectly, in the form of insurance for overseas investment and support for overseas advertising. Comedian Mort Sahl defined these kinds of conservatives as "feeling that they deserve everything they've stolen."

The new grand theft planners in the Republican plutocracy, led by ideologues for the ultra-rich inside the White House, propose as a core of

Bush's tax plan that shareholders who receive corporate dividends should pay only half as much tax.

In 2003, Congress passed an amendment that makes corporate dividends exempt from taxes. Only $20 billion was earmarked for cash-starved states in the 2003 budget. Under the current tax scheme, the legal right-wingers argue, companies have an incentive to not pay dividends. Instead, they amass debt. I asked several liberal economists. All scoffed at the notion that such a move would stimulate the economy. "It might give the stock market a kick in the ass," one said.

The real loser, the US Treasury, would see its income reduced by $100 billion plus over the next decade. This would mean further cuts in social programs, which would hurt the poor. Those possessing large stock port-folios would reap the benefits, of course. But the results would not show up until next year and thus have little chance of tickling the economy now when it needs it.

Talking to people throughout the country over decades, I find that many share my feelings of disgust and loathing over plans to help the rich. So, why don't most Americans vote? Indeed, the majority (some sixty-two percent of eligible voters), according to their massive estrange-ment from the polls in the November 2002 congressional and guberna-torial elections, apparently eschew politics.

I confess that after listening to the car radio and watching the bill-boards, I too became distracted by needs I didn't know I had. The deluge of distracting stimuli muddles the reflective lobes of the brain. The mes-sage of the ads focuses on what you're missing in life.

The AM radio reactionaries rant and rave about the liberal media (practically nonexistent on radio). Their sermon: the rich deserve all they have and more; the poor have had bad luck, inherited poor character, or suffer from stupidity and laziness. Some issues merit much attention: abortion, prayer in school, the alleged right to own as many guns as you can stuff into your house and garage. I hear nothing about the rights to food, shelter, jobs, medical attention, and education.

To stanch the depression reaching me from radio ranters Rush Lim-baugh, Larry Elder, Dr. Laura, and Sean Hannity, I began making a list of peripheral issues featured in bumper stickers and posters. Driving Cali-fornia Highway 395 from Los Angeles to Lone Pine, I spotted a "US out of the UN" sign. I saw numerous "United We Stand" bumper stickers and posters and one that said, "Love your neighbor and don't despair, but keep your fence in good repair."

The "United" slogans come in a red, white, and blue design accompanied by an actual flag decal. Remember John Prine sang, "Your flag decal won't get you into Heaven any more. It's already overcrowded from your last little dirty war."

On the highway, one woman proudly sported an NRA designer license plate. I also passed two firing ranges next to the highway along with several places carved out of the Mojave Desert where you could ride your newest motorized three-wheeler, round and round in the sand, making all the noise you wanted.

I observed two anti-abortion bumper stickers and a sign that advocated prayer in the schools as "the answer." One car's bumper read: "War Is Not the Answer."

"OK," I said to myself, "what is the question?

"Why do I see no indication of budget discussion, the central core of what 'experts' and regular people used to call politics?"

January 2003

2

Classify This!
National Security Culture
Sets the Norm

Two parallel cultures have developed in the post-World War II United States. The "freedom to buy anything" culture coexists with the secret, classified, and downright mysterious national security culture. Even those two words pose a challenge to lexicographers.

The Intelligence Culture
in the National Security Age

Power is the ultimate Aphrodisiac.
—Henry Kissinger

By late June 2003 the Sherlock Holmes unit of the US Army had not encountered the stockpiles of Iraqi weapons of mass destruction that President Bush had assured us constituted an imminent threat to our security.

So, to assuage panic in the White House the CIA began to take the heat. CIA analysts didn't furnish the president with accurate evidence on Iraq's alleged weapons, some White House sources leaked. Critics charged that the Agency had bowed to the president's whim and distorted intelligence to meet political goals. The president, they alleged, wanted to believe that Saddam Hussein had accumulated threatening piles of arms and that he soon planned to supply them to the terrorists who hate us. And the White House even demanded that the CIA furnish the data, whether or not it existed.

CIA Director George Tenet will not testify before some congressional subcommittee that "the White House told us to distort the intelligence so that Bush could justify the war he always intended to wage against Iraq. And we CIA intelligence officials acted obediently as usual. Isn't that our real function—to serve the political wishes of the president in power?" Instead, Tenet will deflect the blame.

Since its inception in 1948 the CIA's foundation contained cracks. "When will Iraqgate surface," I ask myself. High-level officials have already begun tossing around the blame ball like the proverbial hot potato.

Indeed, the June 17, 2003 *BBC News* reports ("Senator Queries WMD Claim") that Michigan Senator Carl Levin, the ranking Democrat on the Senate Armed Services Committee, says he has evidence that the CIA purposely withheld key information from the UN's inspectors deployed in Iraq. There would have been "greater public demand that the inspection process continue," Levin continues, had the public known that the CIA had failed to share its detailed information with the UN inspectors.

"Did the CIA act in this way in order not to undermine [the anti-weapons inspectors] administration policy? Was there another explanation for this?" Levin asked

Instead of trying to answer these rhetorical questions, I recommend that Congress turn the CIA into a branch of the Library of Congress. Don't hold endless strings of congressional inquiries, followed by reports with unheeded recommendations; just send CIA personnel to that wonderful research facility on Capitol Hill.

Look at the current CIA, a "top security" agency. Repeatedly, high officials have sold vital secrets to enemies. In the early 1990s, Aldrich Ames, a trusted Agency bigshot with access to the family jewels, admitted (after being caught) that he had traded burning national secrets for cold cash.

How could the CIA have permitted such lax security, members of Congress wondered, as if greed and treachery only recently arose as characteristics of human behavior? They focused on how and why the CIA let Ames go undetected for years while he conducted his lucrative transactions. But the larger and most obvious questions didn't arise from the hearings: Why should a republic possess so many vital secrets? If they were so vital, how did our government survive after the Soviets learned them?

In the 1980s, Defense Secretary Caspar Weinberger worried publicly that traitors inside US intelligence agencies had already delivered to the Soviets most of our vital national security secrets. Add Ames's top-secret information to those documents pilfered throughout the 1980s and you might well ask: What top secrets remained?

However, possession of these secrets didn't stop the Soviets from collapsing. If Soviet Premier Mikhail Gorbachev's throwing in the towel and refusing to play cold war in the late 1980s resulted from his knowledge of these secrets, then Ames had inadvertently helped end the cold war. If so, maybe Ames deserves a medal, except that he betrayed "our agents," each of whom received a few hundred dollars a month to commit treason against his own country, and then met a traitor's fate.

The Soviets used US "vital secrets," sources, and methods, to discover and dispatch US agents, or Soviet traitors. We did the same to discover agents inside our vital secrets labyrinth. The cold war was about fighting a mortal enemy. Wait! The Soviets proved quite mortal—may their corrupt cold war souls rest in peace.

But remember that Congress created the CIA in the late 1940s for the exclusive purpose of centralizing intelligence to more efficiently combat the Soviet threat. In light of the Soviet demise of more than a decade now, maybe Congress should review the agency's charter.

Such a reappraisal might show that the CIA frequently failed to provide accurate intelligence. Instead, it often provided the documents and rationale to justify policies and agendas designed by a series of presidents.

In the early and mid-1980s CIA Director and "ideologue *über alles*" William Casey directed the CIA to invalidate a former Agency report, citing signs of Soviet weakness, and to conclude instead that the USSR was stronger and more dangerous than ever. Its expansionist posture, the agency dutifully and incorrectly informed the president, demanded that the United States spend ever more money on weapons and covert actions, alongside a propaganda war, to counter the Soviet threat.

The initial report was true. The Soviet apparatus had begun visibly to disintegrate. In the early 1980s, an observant tourist could have testified to the breakdown of production, discipline, and morale throughout the Soviet Union.

The Soviet threat, however, had served for four decades as a pretext for destabilizing elected governments in Iran, Guatemala, and Chile, among others and assassinating people that presidents didn't like, including Patrice Lumumba in the Congo (1960) and Leonidas Trujillo in the Dominican Republic (1961). They never got Fidel.

As a result of some of these "black" operations, the CIA became linked to scandals like the 1970 murder of Chilean Chief of Staff General Rene Schneider and the lurid tales of drug and arms trafficking involved in the 1980s Iran-Contra affair.

The importance of the encompassing Soviet threat allowed the CIA to blithely alter the destiny of other peoples as well as to feed LSD to its own human guinea pigs, one of whom committed suicide. And they spied on Americans abroad and at home.

I know because in 1983 under a Freedom of Information Act request the CIA sent me copies of personal letters I had sent to and received from friends living in the Soviet Union and Cuba. I also received a lengthy personal portrait of my family and me. Millions of Americans could have received similar material from CIA files.

Imagine my surprise then in 1992, when a CIA official telephoned the Institute for Policy Studies where I had worked to request a briefing on ideas about the direction the CIA should take in the future.

For thirty years, IPS had functioned as a center of opposition to the cold war. Its fellows opposed the arms race, US interventions in other nations' affairs, and the very notion of covert action itself. Needless to say, IPS did not approve of government agencies snooping into the lives of US citizens.

Some twenty-five CIA executives arrived, explaining they had requested similar meetings with think tanks of other political stripes as well. Where were politics and economics going? Such a request from a CIA official during the cold war would have shortened his career.

Did these officials fear that the CIA no longer had a *raison d'être*? Did they understand that the Agency belonged exclusively to the cold war and that it therefore had no legitimate charter in the post-Soviet era?

"We've always spoken truth to power," one of our visitors said proudly, referring to the openness the Agency had for opposition points of view.

"But you've also spoken lies to power," I added. "And for more than forty years, the lies have prevailed."

The discussion turned cold. I had insulted them. But the analysts we met seemed like solid researchers who, given a proper atmosphere, could sift and winnow facts and come to reasonable and objective conclusions.

My colleague suggested that maybe the CIA could acquire legitimacy if Congress folded it into the Library of Congress, where in full view of other researchers, professionals could gather data and inform our decision-makers.

Think of the money and embarrassment we'd save by ridding ourselves of the pesky covert and clandestine operations! In the wake of the 9/11 intelligence failure and then the Agency's acquiescence to, or complicity with, White House bullying over the "imminent Iraq threat," the CIA's intelligence mystique has evaporated yet again. It has proven deficient precisely because it kept secret information that should have been public. If we knew the classified information known to a few CIA and FBI agents, we might have helped prevent the 9/11 deeds.

Why shouldn't we know? The terrorists and a few intelligence agents knew. Had we known that the CIA possessed no evidence of Iraqi WMDs, could Bush have convinced the public of the need to go to war?

So, send the CIA to the Library of Congress where its researchers can mingle with the citizens. Imagine a society without hundreds of millions of secrets! Is this crazy? Or, to quote the president, just "revisionist!"

Revised: June 2003

Our Aging Faust

Goethe called his works "one long confession." This desire for psychic purging may have motivated him to write *Faust*, the allegory of every man's fight between conscience and a quest for power.

Faust saves his soul by making a great self-sacrifice, thus nullifying his contract with the Devil. Only in self-denial does he find fulfillment.

Compare Goethe's literary hero with our contemporary, aging Faust, Bob McNamara, writing, "the book I planned never to write."

The purpose of his 1995 memoir, *In Retrospect: The Tragedy and Lessons of Vietnam* (Times Books, New York) McNamara says, is to "put before the American people why their government and its leaders behaved as they did and what we may learn from their experience." In *The Fog of War*, a 2003 documentary film, McNamara repeats the statements he made in the book. Not just to free himself from three decades of accumulated guilt does McNamara use public space to simultaneously flail and defend himself.

"I have grown sick at heart," he writes, "witnessing the cynicism and even contempt with which so many people view our political institutions and leaders."

But McNamara's memoir will only increase that cynicism and contempt. How will parents of dead soldiers or civilians, Vietnamese or American, feel when they read that as early as 1966 McNamara had become "increasingly skeptical of our ability to achieve our political objectives in Vietnam through military means." Nevertheless, he continues, "this did not diminish my involvement in the shaping of Vietnam policy."

Defense Secretary in the 1960s and memoir writer in the 1990s, McNamara still gropes for the elusive coherence that can offer a graceful endgame for his life. The Great Administrator, who examined as if they were business reports the daily mounting body counts, spread of antiwar protests, and requests for more US troops to embark for Vietnam, recalls that "1966 began with an event that deeply depressed me."

The next sentence should refer to a Pentagon request to use nuclear weapons, or reports on the increasing drug use by GIs. Instead, the depressing event involves an original member of the best and brightest: "MacGeorge Bundy left the Administration."

This emotional revelation offers insight into McNamara's moral learning disability, that ethical gap that allowed him to order missions of death without questioning his own integrity. Bundy was a pillar of stability, one of the solid crowd of patriots and intellects that reinforced McNamara when he authorized "Westy" (General William Westmoreland) to send more troops and when he lied to the public by declaring he saw "light at the end of the tunnel."

McNamara acknowledges his doldrums over the loss of a colleague, but remains detached from the massive loss of life in "McNamara's War."

When Norman Morrison burned himself to death to protest the war in front of McNamara's Pentagon window as the Buddhist monks did in Vietnam, McNamara says he "reacted to the horror of his action by bottling up my emotions and avoided talking about them with anyone, even my family. I knew Marg and our three children shared many of Morrison's feelings about the war, as did the wives and children of several of my cabinet colleagues. And I believed I shared some of these thoughts. There was much that Marg and I and the children should have talked about, yet at moments like this I often turn inward instead—it is a grave weakness." McNamara senses that his soul was at stake, but the glimmers of humane feelings that he allowed himself to acknowledge confronted a stronger deeper commitment, one that cast a shadow over his ability to see right and wrong.

Despite his deep doubts about the war's winnability (based on his assessment of numbers, body counting, and other military measuring instruments), McNamara continued to support it publicly because of his loyalty to the president and because he interpreted his constitutional oath to include obedience to presidential dictates. This former automobile company CEO is heart and soul a servant.

After making his business assessment that the war is unprofitable, McNamara makes his moral judgment: that it is therefore wrong. But unlike the robot accountant who cannot draw moral lines between what the figures dictate and human factors, McNamara understands that there is a choice. Torn between conscience over lost American lives (tens of thousands of people he doesn't know) on the one hand and his sense of duty to serve American power (people he knows and respects) on the other, McNamara chose power over conscience. And he stuck with that choice for twenty-five years, until he saw the end of the cold war as making it permissible for him to reveal his doubts.

But the fact remains: McNamara gave the orders to kill. His behavior cost millions of lives and led to the agony of prolonged war. McNamara presents himself as a morally strong man, but his memoir indicates he couldn't confront the inherent dilemma of making imperial policies inside a formal democracy, of using imperial reasoning inside a republican form of government. His book does not review the relevant history, 1945, for example, when the French stole Vietnam's independence, or 1954, when the United States nullified the Geneva Treaty and negated the will of the Vietnamese majority. Even Eisenhower admitted in his memoirs that had a vote been taken, Ho Chi Minh would have received eighty percent. McNamara, at times brutally self-critical, remains in his political thinking an unacknowledged imperialist.

I'm glad he wrote his personal testimony to the deceit of the past. But one must proceed with caution about the lessons he teaches us. McNamara's view of life as a series of successes and failures reduces history to short-term problem solving. McNamara sinned and seeks atonement. But the depth of his evil still eludes him. He does not say that our nation should have had no interest in defeating an insurrectionary force in Vietnam or that US security was in fact ill-served by promoting such an endeavor.

His memoir thus misses the very moral focus he desires because he cannot separate morality from notions of success and failure. He still believes "the United States of America fought in Vietnam for eight years for what it believed to be good and honest reasons ... to protect our security, prevent the spread of totalitarian communism, and promote individual freedom and political democracy."

Such clichés in defense of so much killing! The aims are noble, but the strategy had little chance to succeed. To remain as defense secretary he had to ignore the incongruities between the trite expression of goals and the bestiality required to achieve them. He pressed on, "ravaging a beautiful country and sending young Americans to their death year after year, because they [the war planners] had no other plan." The war could have and should have been halted, McNamara concedes, but he and other Johnson senior advisers failed to do so "through ignorance, inattention, flawed thinking, political expediency, and lack of courage."

Yes, lack of courage! There is a logic of intervention that required top officials to insulate themselves, to place a wall between the questions that should arise when bombing missions are ordered, for example, against cities. McNamara does not acknowledge the interventionist logic because he doesn't see himself as an imperialist. His self-image is of the hard-headed fact man in the service of decent people, a member of a fraternity of trustees and gentry, in high command, from whose loyalty society achieves stability and integrity.

The antiwar activists chanted, "Hey, hey, LBJ. How many kids did you kill today?" stinging President Johnson and McNamara. Indeed, McNamara's own family raised serious questions. The demonstrators by the millions marched, carried placards that read, "U.S. OUT OF VIETNAM". Few suspected that McNamara secretly agreed with their assessment. He felt he could not confront the Cabinet hawks and then demand that President Johnson admit error and withdraw. That is not what an imperial adviser does.

So millions of Vietnamese died; 58,000 Americans fell; another half-million returned with physical or mental war wounds that endure. Now, the cold war over, victims and their relatives discover that had McNamara possessed the honesty, integrity, and courage to stop it, the war might not have continued past 1966.

Ironically, in recognition of his performance as Defense Secretary for Kennedy and Johnson, McNamara was appointed head of the World Bank. That's life in Empire City, where nothing succeeds like failure.

McNamara avoids the word "empire" to describe the US world position. As World Bank president, he defined his role as bringing development and allaying the burdens of third-world poverty, not running a bank through which giant corporations got roads built to bring raw materials from mines and plantations to port.

McNamara's Bank meant progress, not damming nature to provide cheap power for multinational enterprises, and making loans that made fragile third-world independence even more precarious.

McNamara, enjoying the privileges and comforts of the elite, does not offer himself for trial for crimes against humanity, barbaric deeds for which he is as guilty as the Nazi leaders tried after World War II.

Instead, McNamara expiates his guilt with a mea culpa. It works. One of his former associates said, "Poor Bob, he's carried this burden for so many years." Poor Bob, indeed.

Now that at age 87, McNamara has let his emotions spill out of their shell and onto the public's lap, he may feel better. But what have President George W. Bush and his advisers learned from his memoirs? The unscrupulous continue to counsel the amoral Crown. The Secretary of

State lacks the courage to demand the King change his erroneous course. Like McNamara, Colin Powell plays the obedient servant to power. Recall that Cyrus Vance resigned and set an example for integrity because he understood that President Carter's hare-brained "rescue" mission in Iran could lead to truly devastating consequences.

In his book, McNamara strives for grace, citing T.S. Eliot's *Four Quartets*: "And last the rending pain of reenactment/Of all that you have done and been; the shame/Of motives late revealed, and the awareness/Of things ill done and done to others' harm/Which once you took for exercise of virtue."

The repentant but still strangely arrogant McNamara might better have used Faust's words. "The worm am I, that in the dust does creep."

In all fairness, however, McNamara stands as a veritable model of morality when placed against the moral retards that have governed the country since 1980. He at least now recognizes the nature of morality in public office, in contrast to the armadillo-like shell placed over the sensibilities of the Bush administration.

April 2004

Bob McNamara felt that he couldn't tell the public what he knew about the impossibility of winning the Vietnam War. He tried to serve two masters: the American public, to whom he was supposedly accountable, and the national security elite, led by the President. McNamara's behavior as Secretary of Defense raises the question of whether morality can exist inside a national security state that poses as a republic.

A Panglossian Conversation

Thanks to Washington being the leakiest capital in the world, the media discovered that in August 2001 US intelligence reported to President Bush that some of the fiends linked to Osama bin Laden had (1) enrolled in flying schools and (2) might skyjack a jumbo jet. Not only did members of our intelligence have solid information that something deeply evil was afoot, but two years before, sources from the Library of Congress had given the CIA information that the terrorists might well use the large planes as explosive weapons.

More telling, two months before the fatal events of 9/11, a Phoenix-based FBI Special Agent, an acknowledged expert on terrorism, had even put those pieces of information together and predicted exactly the kind of scenario that White House officials claim no one could have predicted. Bin Laden or whoever did the planning for the affluent zealot would slip his suicide squads into flight schools and then do the unthinkable, the unimaginable—use passenger-filled planes as incendiary bombs.

Information reached the FBI that the Muslim pupils showed no interest in how to take off or land; only in steering the craft once airborne. In short, information galore existed that the FBI might have employed to avert the horrendous events of 9/11.

So, citizens and amateur detectives ask the famous questions: who knew what, when did they know it, and what should they have done? This potential Washington scandal has reanimated some of my friends who still blame Green Party candidate Ralph Nader for W's ascendancy to the White House. Most of my friends deny that Bush won the election. Some of the more conspiracy-minded have even suggested that the artless and illegitimate Bush and the crafty Dick Cheney may have plotted the whole 9/11 disaster (with Israel, of course) in order to remake the world, increase their power, and make large profits.

I dismiss this kind of explanation as bordering on paranoia. Having spent 25 years in Washington, I prefer the more obvious and bureaucratic explanation for the fact that the White House did nothing after FBI and CIA officials had advised Bush of the bizarre and frightening facts they had uncovered prior to that fatal day.

I asked Dr. Slick E. Pangloss, a White House insider known for his fast talking and eternal optimism, about what Bush actually understood in August when the CIA briefed him at his Crawford, Texas ranch that bin Laden's fiends might skyjack planes and use them as weapons.

"When Bush heard the CIA's report," Pangloss said, "he appeared confused and muttered that he could sure use a drink. Everyone in the room was quiet. The CIA also gave him written reports with long lists of policy recommendations including alerting the airlines and the pilots, increasing security at the airports, arresting the suspected terrorists, and, well, lots of things that cops and bureaucrats would think of that would give them more jobs and power and prestige."

"Did Bush read the reports," I asked.

"Are you kidding?" my straight-talking source replied. "Bush doesn't read reports longer than a few paragraphs. Do you think we're dealing with another Bill Clinton, a man who would absorb accurately humongous amounts of written and oral information and then lie about them to the public? A president who knows less can cause less damage."

"So," I persisted, "what happened next?"

Bush did exactly what his father and mother had told him to do in a situation where he didn't know what to do and felt like taking a drink but couldn't go to the gym. He phoned Uncle Dick Cheney."

"And?"

"Uncle Dick, who for decades had been privy to Washington alarmism, told the president to relax and do a three-hour workout at the ranch. He ridiculed the idea that anyone would skyjack a plane and fly it into a strategic target. He reminded W that the business of the administration was business, especially the oil and weapons business, in which both the Bush and Cheney families had substantial interests, and not to get distracted by so-called intelligence reports."

"But," I asked, "wouldn't it have been prudent to at least tell the pilots and flight attendants about the possible threats, make the cockpit doors more secure and maybe even alert the public?"

"Are you out of your mind?" Pangloss asked. "That kind of policy would have led to panic. People would have cancelled their flights, their vacations, and even their shopping sprees. It could have led to ruin.

Imagine what the Democrats would have said. They would have accused W of paranoia. Rumors would have spread that he had begun drinking again. No way we could have followed that scenario."

"But," I insisted, "members of our own intelligence community predicted that something terrible was about to happen."

"First," he snapped, "the FBI didn't bother to send that report to the White House. Second, who ever believes the words of spies? When you say intelligence, are we talking about signal intelligence or photo intelligence? Those sources rely on technology and therefore merit our credibility. Human intelligence, that's the lowest source on the reliability totem pole. You recall that Stalin had placed Count Sorge, a top agent, in the Nazi Embassy in Tokyo. Sorge, as German Ambassador to Japan, had one task: find out whether Japan planned to attack the Soviet Union from the Manchurian border. If not, Stalin could move a million troops from their posts there to the German front where they were desperately needed.

"Stalin, however, didn't believe the word of a spy. He kept the troops where they were, his armies fighting the Nazis suffered incredible casualties and Count Sorge was discovered and executed."

"Are you saying," I continued, "that like Stalin our leaders dismissed vital information because they didn't believe in human intelligence? Is this what Republicans do?"

"Was John F. Kennedy a Republican?" he asked. "US officials got wind of Soviet missiles in Cuba in August 1962 from a very reliable French spy, but Kennedy dismissed the reports. Once again, he didn't trust human intelligence. He didn't take action to counter Soviet missiles in Cuba until he saw the aerial photographs."

"Hold on," I said, "by the mid-1990s the FBI had ample information about Al Qaeda operatives enrolling in our flight-training schools, that French authorities had caught some Islamic nut just before he flew a plane into the Eiffel Tower, that the guys who rammed their explosives-laden truck into the World Trade Center in 1993 had also discussed suicide missions using skyjacked planes. When does the alarm bell ring with this president?"

"Take it easy," Pangloss warned. "You're stepping into dangerous territory. The president didn't know the attack was coming. In fact, look at the confusion that ensued after the 9/11 bombings. He boarded Air Force One in a daze and then no one knew where to take him."

"But that hasn't stopped him from selling photos of himself on Air

Force One talking on the phone on that fatal day with Dick Cheney, for $5000 smackers apiece."

"Hey," said Pangloss, "that's just politics. Gore would've done the same thing."

"What was he asking Cheney anyway?" I inquired.

"He was asking Cheney if it was still too dangerous to come back to Washington," he replied.

"It sounds to me," I concluded, "that the administration had the necessary facts and didn't act on them for whatever reason and now we should stop this bipartisan game and demand explanations."

"You know," Dr. Pangloss replied, "your persistent questioning of our leaders' motives can only throw division into our up-to-now united public opinion. You're beginning to sound downright unpatriotic. I may have to give your name to Attorney General Ashcroft."

May 2002

Ashcroft has followed in a long tradition of repressive officials. The 1798 Alien and Sedition Acts, four laws enacted by Congress, gave President John Adams the power to imprison or deport aliens suspected of activities posing a threat to the national government. Using the façade of "hostility" from France's revolutionary government, the Federalist-controlled Congress actually aimed to undermine Thomas Jefferson, the leader of the Republican Party. The laws postponed citizenship for newly arrived immigrants, the core of Jefferson's voting strength. Although President Adams did not use the Alien Acts, their passage did impose a chilling effect on the country. The Sedition Act virtually nullified the First Amendment by making it a crime to criticize the government.

Between 1918 and 1921, Woodrow Wilson's attorney general, A. Mitchell Palmer, staged his infamous raids against supposedly subversive immigrants. In the post-World War II period, "McCarthyism" enveloped a broad-based repression in which all branches of the government with cooperation from corporate and union leaders cracked down on communists, pinkos, fellow travelers, and, liberals themselves. In each period, however, defenders of the Bill of Rights fought the repression, using their knowledge of history and the long struggle to establish basic rights as the pillar of their arguments.

History? What's That?

As I tried to explain to my class about the tradition of individual rights and the various attempts of the executive branch to usurp various and sundry of those rights over the years, I had just gotten to the subject of Watergate when one of my students' cell phones rang to the opening bars of "Für Elise." The student apologized for forgetting to turn his phone off. I excused him, remarking that Elise surely must have felt flattered to have had a song written to her by the genius Ludwig van Beethoven. "And," I added, "this tune plays every few seconds or even more frequently on mobile telephones around the world. Hey, what status-minded student would be caught without a cell phone?"

My student stared at me, not locating Elise, Beethoven (maybe a guy on a Beatles song?), or Watergate, the point where I stopped my discourse.

A few of the students did know about Beethoven and even about Elise, the woman who inspired the song. Some even had heard or read about the Watergate break-in on June 17, 1972, but none could explain it. Indeed, to this day, only the burglars themselves and those who commanded the White House plumbers know why they raided Democratic National Committee headquarters, a felony that led to the greatest presidential scandal in US history. "Yes," I explained, "even more important than the Monica-Paula Jones-Whitewater themes combined."

Richard M. Nixon, as Oliver Stone's film by that title makes clear, had a criminal mentality. He wanted his plumbers to commit crimes, like breaking into the Brookings Institution to find incriminating documents on his enemies, or siccing the IRS on his political foes. As we later discovered, Nixon organized the so-called plumbers, some of whom were extreme right-wing anti-Castro Cubans, to stop the leaks. He feared that disloyal members of his staff would pass policy information to the media, including a planned opening to China, and thus interfere with his secret agendas. Henry Kissinger, his national security adviser and later secretary of state, shared these phobias about openness. If accountability existed, meaning that the Executive shared its policies with the legislature, Congress might discover, for example, that Nixon and Kissinger had ordered the secret bombing of Cambodia beginning in 1969.

Nixon, a lawyer, showed little concern for the rule of law. His close advisers also displayed extreme contempt for citizens' rights. The late 1960s and early 1970s were still the age of COINTELPRO, the FBI's illegal infiltration into the civil rights and antiwar movements. Nixon had ordered his plumbers to break into the office of Daniel Ellsberg's psychiatrist. Ellsberg had delivered the Pentagon Papers to the *New York Times* and Nixon had hoped to get some dirt on the "s.o.b." as he called Ellsberg.

But with Jimmy Carter, in 1977, the United States restored some equilibrium between runaway imperial power and those republican principles that act as delicate bookends to hold our fragile national stack together. Presidents Reagan and Bush (41), however, eroded Carter's clean human rights guidelines, as did Clinton in his eight years. "National Security," that dreaded and enigmatic phrase, always popped out of the mouths of officials to justify more phone taps, less government openness, and more contempt for the Bill of Rights. The process of empire, running overseas operations without express congressional approval, had encroached on meaningful due process of law.

Then came 9/11 and in the terrifying new atmosphere that emerged from it, I found it ever more difficult to explain to students why Nixon's Watergate caper frightened so many Americans in the 1970s, and sent so many high White House officials to prison, for the break-in crime itself or for covering up the escapade.

"Nixon's lack of respect for law endangered all of us," I preached. But, looking back, I see Watergate as a relatively minor threat to civil liberties compared to the action of our current government. In the 1972 *Washington Post*, reporters Bob Woodward and Carl Bernstein informed the public that they had traced a routine break-in at an office building to the highest offices in the land. Their media rivals tried to get other scoops. A young CBS reporter, Dan Rather, asked Nixon tough questions and took the mud that the powerful throw at journalists who lose their ovine qualities, including suggestions that their actions showed not just lack of respect for the president, but possibly anti-patriotic sentiments as well.

Members of both houses of Congress investigated the Watergate hanky-panky and public opinion rallied behind them to force the truth into the open, despite pleas of national security from the White House. Watergate started with the 1972 arrest of burglars, in search presumably of documents that might have compromised the president. It ended with the August 1974 resignation of Richard Nixon.

"Watch out," I warn the students. "Watergate was terrible and now is worse. The arrest of an American hoodlum named José Padilla[1] could have an impact not on George W. Bush's career but on your lives." They stare at me as if I'm either an alarmist or a coddler of terrorists. "I don't know if Padilla did or didn't conspire to make a dirty bomb and detonate it," I say, "but I do know that he can't see his lawyer. That makes me suspicious of our government.

"Imagine yourselves," I say, "US citizens, being arrested and charged with being enemy combatants and placed into what *New York Times* columnist Bob Herbert called 'a procedural black hole' ("Isn't Democracy Worth It?," June 17, 2002). That's a place in the United States (a Navy brig in South Carolina, not Camp X-ray in Guantánamo Bay, Cuba) in which legal rights cease to exist, where the Constitution does not apply."

In our legal system, as the administration has interpreted it, the Justice Department does not have to charge Padilla nor produce evidence that warrants his detention. They can hold him indefinitely because, under the new administration guidelines, people like Padilla have virtually no rights.

This terrifies me, as does the treatment of John Walker Lindh,[2] whatever he might have done with the Taliban, whom he joined before the United States invaded Afghanistan. If Padilla conspired with Al Qaeda terrorists why not present the evidence and charge him with conspiracy to commit mass murder?

My teachers drilled into my head that we lived in a country of law, not of men. The law must always dictate because men's passion, good or bad, can run away with them and lead to tyranny, even with the best of intentions.

When I was younger, I mouthed those sentiments, but never really thought about them. They sounded like other clichés we learned during those heady World War II years when patriotism dictated that teachers stress democracy in its fullest forms and, of course, equality. "Don't forget," my third-grade teacher explained, "we Americans are all equal and one American equals ten Japs."

Well, no system is perfect! But during World War II we understood our Nazi and Japanese enemies and the advantages of our system over theirs. Those differences made our patriotic feelings intense. As imperfect as our democracy seemed, with racial segregation still intact, we still stood on a set of principles from which we could do battle with our enemies abroad and with our own imperfections at home.

Without that platform of freedom, of absolutely inviolable rights, we become a government of men, some of them quite smarmy. It might not be long before a man with a criminal mind like Nixon once again commands. One meaning of Watergate is that our media could report, our lawyers could invoke the law, Congress could deliberate, and the citizens could understand a complex legal process. Thanks to the media's exposure of executive wrongdoing, Congress forced the president and his staff to become accountable for their actions. The media have grown more timid since Watergate, as secret government has proliferated. It's as if each prospective investigative journalist now possesses a self-censoring mechanism that rings like an alarm bell: will this story get me into career trouble around the patriotism issue? Will an editor accuse me of undermining the war effort if I show high officials having lied or engaged in hanky-panky. Will I wear the label "soft on terrorists?"

The war against terrorism (war against an abstraction?) has taken parallel and aggressive tracks to those ridden by the terrorists themselves. Terrorism makes us frightened and as fear temporarily overcomes confidence in our tradition of rights, at least in a sector of the public, men in the administration act to remove traditional freedoms under the aegis of fighting the covert terrorists. Under the leadership of the self-righteous George W. Bush and his puritanical Attorney General John Ashcroft, the threats to liberties have risen beyond the level of the Nixon Administration.

Watch out, fellow citizens and "all the ships at sea" as an old radio commentator once said. This war on terrorism could end up terrorizing all of us.

The class ends. Students turn on their cell phones. "Für Elise" and "La Cucaracha" alert them that their girlfriends or bookies are on the line. So much for a history lesson!

June 2002

3

Sheep Don't Need Whipping:
Media in the Twenty-First Century

The government stores history in a partitioned attic. The national secu-rity section holds hundreds of millions of super-secret, "classified" documents. The public side gets dragged down once a year. It contains some revolutionary events such as the Boston Tea Party and copies of Tom Paine's Common Sense. *Except for national holidays, like July 4, the media have become the national source of memory. Indeed, every five, ten, and twenty-five years, we get reminded about important events of the past—well, some of them.*

World News in Shotgun Pellets
of Anxiety from the Media

Did the extra cup of coffee or the TV news cause my anxiety? Or should I attribute my uneasiness to the news headlines blaring over my car radio as I brake to a stop on a ten-lane Los Angeles freeway? The media will report any "news" that might produce anxiety in the reader, listener, or viewer. Like my fellow sufferers from exposure to untold dangers and impending calamities, I look for redress in shopping (even if only for Prozac). I don't want to sound like a paranoid schizophrenic, but I sometimes suspect that the mass media intend their news as a means to induce shopping behavior. Just because of who pays the bills for the news!

The mass media, for example, report uncritically on a government official's remarks that scare people. Still reeling from the 9/11 attacks, the public now learns that it must fear a new form of terrorism. On May 6, 2002, John R. Bolton, the Under Secretary of State for Arms Control, "revealed" that US intelligence has concluded that Cuba possesses a biological weapons capacity and, worse, has shared this germ warfare technology with other "rogue states." This publicized accusation colored the atmosphere for former President Jimmy Carter's visit to Cuba and provided a right-wing, pro-embargo context for all discussion of the Cuba issue for the next few weeks. It also terrified the less-enlightened citizens.

The media gave immense amounts of space to Bolton's undocumented accusation and, days later, offered only a few lines to Cuban President Fidel Castro's strong denial. In order to win big space in the media, I suppose Fidel would have had to say, "If Bolton doesn't retract that outrageous lie, we'll spray him and his whole family."

I feel as if I get sprayed daily with pellets of media information, true or false, but always incomplete. The media spew annoying and constant data. I take it in the eyes, ears, and brain.

Since he produced no facts, I assume that Bolton's charge against Cuba had political motives. Bolton belongs to the anti-Castro gang that wants Bush to "do something" about Cuba. But to what do we attribute the mass media's coverage of transportation and natural disasters in the third world? Transportation disaster stories tend to increase anxiety levels while simultaneously creating mysteries that the media leave unsolved.

In the second week of May 2002, for example, yet another Haitian boat (how many can you recall?) loaded with migrants sank. The boat was overloaded, the press reported. The newspapers and TV don't explain why so many Haitians boarded an overloaded boat. Presumably, they were bound for Florida. Should we conclude from the report that Haitians are desperate and therefore undesirable as immigrants? Or, we get responses such as "Oh well, it was only Haitians," as if dying at sea somehow relates to one's being Haitian. We get no insight into the nature of Haitian poverty, or the role the United States played in the internal affairs of that impoverished island for the last two centuries.

A May 4 *Los Angeles Times* fourteen-line article reports that a ferry in Bangladesh capsized in a storm with four hundred people aboard. Police feared hundreds had died. "As many as 100 people were reported to have swum to shore or were picked up by other boats." Then, you learn an apparently important detail: "The ferry sank nearly two hours into the trip from Dhaka, the capital, to Patuakhlai, 95 miles south." Since a few of us might not know exactly how to pinpoint these locations on the map, the mention of the names of these places can increase our anxiety and sense of ignorance. God, we should know about the places where all those people died! Maybe we should try Mapquest?

The *New York Times* ran a similar, slightly longer story the next day. Neither story said why the ferry capsized. Both implied that a storm had caused the tragedy. Yet storms don't cause the capsizing of the Vancouver-Seattle ferry or the passenger ships that cross Lake Michigan. Was this storm so powerful that it simply knocked the boat over? Was the ferry captain drunk and maybe steered the ship into a reef? Was the ferry unsafe because of poor construction or poor maintenance? Did it not have enough life rafts? Well, I could go on guessing. But how good it feels to shop for something you don't need or want after digesting the bare details of a massive catastrophe.

How many short accounts have we perused of fatal train wrecks in India or Bangladesh, buses going over cliffs in Peru killing fifty passengers and twenty chickens, and ferries sinking in the Philippines with hundreds drowning? Rarely do we learn the cause of the mishap. Should we assume that third-world drivers and pilots have less competence than those that steer our public vehicles, or that third-world trains, buses, and boats are poorly maintained?

One of my students concluded from reading such short accounts of calamities that "God doesn't seem to bless" third-world people or they lack adequate disaster relief agencies. The implied message in these tragedies is: think twice about taking any ground or sea transportation in the third world and thank the Lord that we have a National Transportation Safety Board to impose safety standards on public vehicles.

The mass media rarely report about how systemic pressures by those who manage the world economy have forced third-world farmers to substitute cut flowers and macadamia nuts for corn, beans, and other staples. Nor do we learn about how such policies have led to hunger and even starvation in Africa and Latin America. Predictably, the media do run "famine" stories, as if Africans have either bad karma or have screwed up their economies. Rarely do the media explain hunger as a result of World Bank and IMF-enforced policies.[1]

Similarly, the deforestation of the third world, for industrial wood use, chopsticks, and packing cases, has also led to climate changes and, in turn, droughts and floods.

To this day, IMF and World Bank experts lecture third-world peasants, those who have fed the world for millennia, on how they should forego planting their traditional crops, which they know about and with which they can feed themselves and, instead, try to attract foreign investors, supposedly to benefit their national economies. Yet the experts fail to address the established character of foreign capital, which has proven to be more fickle in its behavior than Hollywood movie stars.

The media eschew complicated explanations about the roots of large-scale tragedies. They prefer to stick to the gory facts and readers or viewers can draw whatever implications they wish.

How can one draw logical conclusions from shotgun blasts of data? The newspapers and TV set priorities. They give tiny space to a ferry tragedy that claims hundreds of lives in Bangladesh and several pages to the deaths of three people when a Los Angeles commuter train collides with an oncoming freight train. In early May 2002, the *Los Angeles Times* headlined the case of a thirty-three-year-old Southern California teacher who ran off to Nevada for a day with a fifteen-year-old student.

"Local news demands space," a veteran reporter scolded me. And how many Bangladeshis live in the Los Angeles area? What are a few hundred dead Asians compared to a homegrown sex scandal?

Ironically, the US population has become ever more third world in origin. Do newspaper publishers and TV news executives still assume that their South Asian readers and viewers care little about following up on reports of loss of life from that part of the world?

Despite the existence of a large population of Korean origin in Southern California, the *Los Angeles Times* did not cover a late April UN warning that mass starvation looms in North Korea unless that government receives additional funding for food supplies. Indeed, as Sam Smith reports in the May 3 *Progressive Review*, UN aid officials said in early May that the World Food Program, UNICEF, and the UN Office for the Coordination of Humanitarian Affairs had issued a joint statement that more than six million North Koreans face acute shortages of food, medicine, and drinking water.

The papers and TV provided regular and critical coverage about the breakdown of the façade of democracy in Zimbabwe as President Robert Mugabe patently rigged his recent re-election effort. Reports abounded about unfair attacks on opposition candidates, the censoring of the press, and the intimidation of honest judges. But the same papers have provided scant coverage of the current drought in Zimbabwe where five and a half million children face serious food shortages.

Nor have the major media covered the warning from the World Food Program that the 2.6 million people it is currently feeding in Southern Africa could double in a short time because of harsh weather conditions, economic and political instability, and the spread of HIV/AIDS. "The situation is extremely critical," said WFP regional director Judith Lewis.

Or, we learn from the *New York Times* that the extreme right in England has won a few local elections, but read nothing about an impending famine in Sudan. Food and Agriculture Organization Director General Jacques Diouf called on representatives of countries participating in the twenty-seventh FAO Regional Conference for Latin America and the Caribbean in Havana to intensify efforts against hunger, which afflicts fifty-four million people in the region. No report of this in the big media!

Large-scale accidents and procedural rights violations certainly merit coverage, but why emphasize those stories to the detriment of massive starvation reports that governments could respond to and rapidly supply food? Since sensitive people would certainly show concern about reports of massive starvation, I would assume that the media would feature them. It couldn't hurt shopping patterns! My mother assumed that she could increase my appetite as a child by filling me with gory details of starving children in China.

Behind the selection of what gets reported and what doesn't, lies, among other factors, the accessibility of the tragedy site to news photographers. TV news editors have concluded that without pictures it's hard to keep an audience's attention, so it's best to minimize such stories.

Yet, in the so-called information age, TV news has claimed a right to present its version of "the world tonight" as serious discourse, albeit it reveals it in an entertainment format. Newspapers try to compete with such packaging by juicing up their stories with color photos.

Reflect on Aldous Huxley's warning in *Brave New World* that when the prestigious fountains of information burlesque our culture they also threaten to shrink and trivialize it. When a right-wing ideologue like John Bolton issues an alarming but undocumented allegation about Cuba's supposed biological warfare potential, the reporters should have asked him for proof. Bolton, like other ultra-reactionaries who occupy high positions in the administration, understands that in an atmosphere of mindless reporting on third-world threats or accidents, he can with a dramatic sound-bite spin the media in his direction. The public's right to know the facts, the reporter's job, doesn't enter into either Bolton's or the news editors' criteria for making news. By treating the world's events in scandalous modes the media both trivialize and thus distort. But above and beyond those sins, the media turn news into anxiety, packaged, of course, as entertainment.

So, don't blame all of your daily worries on the caffeine in your morning coffee.

May 2002

Religious Diversion from the Issues in the Age of Reason and Hi Tech

The Pope has taken the lead among religious heavies in speaking out about the transcendent issues of our time. He has attacked corporate globalization for increasing the disparity between rich and poor. He has berated the commercialization of life as toxic to the human spirit. He has declared the Church on the side of the poor and suffering masses of the world. Imagine, amidst all of his inspiring messages, he has to face the facts that his holy soldiers, the parish priests, and even some bishops have, how shall I put it, gone a tad beyond breaking their vows of chastity.

In order to restore order to a Church whose clergy finds itself enmeshed in sex perversion scandals, the Vatican has declared a "zero tolerance" policy for priests' sexual practices. This means, I suppose, that priests can no longer even check the kids for hernias and hemorrhoids like they did when I was a kid (I knew this from kids in Catholic schools).

Then again, I've yet to see any authority announce say, a five- or even ten-percent level of tolerance for drugs, so why should we expect one on sex? Some Philippine priest who parents say regularly wrestled with their kids, claimed that Americans couldn't understand this harmless behavior because of "cultural differences."

Well, the Church is nothing if not absolute. The Pope has always demanded that priests' vows include abstention from all sex. I assume that the Pope abstained when he was a priest. Well, at least we haven't heard of any sex abuse charges filed against him.

So, I concluded zero tolerance means not just that priests can no longer diddle kids and stay priests, they can't even make it with adults, bishops will no longer cover up their pederasty, and cardinals will no longer protect the trysting activities of bishops. After two-thousand-plus years, as corporate managers direct their world of globalization that has excluded some three billion people, the Church must face the fact that priests, like other people, have sex. Some are homosexuals, some heterosexuals, and some simply depraved. All the traditional, rock-solid singing, chanting, and fabulous architecture now looks so fragile, because of a sex scandal that has growing international proportions.

Moral issues of a different sort have emerged among the rabbinate. The insertion of Israel into the world has challenged the ethics of Judaism. Although we have not seen widespread accusations of rabbis shtupping bar mitzvah students, we have heard them defend outrageous Israeli behavior. There are important exceptions to this statement, but while newspaper ads to "defend Israel" occupy pages in the leading US newspapers, we have not seen an equivalent number of rabbis speak against the preaching of racial hatred that has become rampant in everyday conversation among Jews in the United States and Israel.

Some rabbis encourage fanatics to build settlements on the West Bank even now, while much of the world condemns Israel's takeover of other people's land. These rabbis insist, like kids playing turf games, "It's ours. We were here first," referring to biblical citations over the millennia. Leading members of the rabbinate justify the demolition (bulldozing) of other people's houses without judicial procedure.

"We love Israel," chant pro-Israel demonstrators in New York and Los Angeles. They left out "right or wrong." Just as some perverted priests have stained the reputation of the Church, so too Israeli Prime Minister Ariel Sharon gives Judaism a bad name. He has removed ethics and substituted state loyalty, except that in his mind the Israeli state has become an ever-expanding entity. Jews who occupy and kill become national heroes. Why have a most historically minded people not looked at Israel as the last settler colony of the twentieth century? Why don't Jews compare Sharon's plan for blocking contiguous Palestinian territory on the West Bank to that of the former apartheid government of South Africa, intent on creating Bantustan-like territories for the Palestinians?

If we look to the Protestant clergy for leadership in advancing a world agenda that copes with the demanding issues of the day, we encounter nasty stories about the most famous of all Protestants, Billy Graham, passing anti-Semitic remarks to his pal Richard Nixon.

The TV ministers divert us from the issues of our time. Jerry Falwell and Pat Robertson make PR for Israel, while ignoring war, racism, occupation, and the consumption of ever more electronic and electrical goods whose production exacerbates global warming and encourages worldwide income disparity.

Unlike Rev. Graham, whose anti-Semitism was recorded in a private conversation with President Nixon, some of the Israel-loving televangelists make their anti-Semitism public.

When a rabbi called Texan Rev. James Roberson an anti-Semite for saying that God didn't hear Jews' prayers and for advising his flock to be wary of doing business with Jews, Roberson denied he disliked Jews. "An anti-Semite," he declared, "that's someone who hates Jews more than he's supposed to."

Ironically, those who used to spout anti-Semitism from the pulpit like Old Faithful belched sulfur water, now promote Israeli territorial expansion. For history to turn out right, as the Bible supposedly says, the Hebrews must occupy what would be greater Israel. They chant this mantra with their demands to outlaw abortions, legalize prayer in schools, and extend the death penalty to ever more crimes.

In the late 1970s and early 1980s, Israeli Prime Minister Menachem Begin gave the Star of David as gifts to several of the ultra-right evangelists for defending Israel. Like Begin, these fundamentalists believed that all American Jews should go to Israel.

So, powerful religious leaders—not all of them, thank God—like the world's political class, don't have an agenda to address the raging wars and weapons production. They couldn't even agree on the feeble 1997 Kyoto accords to protect the environment, which deteriorates daily before our eyes.

Our leaders divert us, albeit it is not entertaining. George W. Bush takes Saudi Prince Abdullah for a ride in his pickup truck and feels good because they saw a wild turkey. Instead of spiritual leadership at the pulpit, we have pederasts throughout the ranks of the priesthood, and leading Protestants advising the president to oppose stem cell research.

As empire pushes ever outward, knocking down people and Nature in search of profit and control, we find ourselves bereft of spiritual and political leaders. We have been thrown back on ourselves, our communities, our own collective spirituality to join with those few who continue to speak from the pulpit and political podium to protect our sanity against the ever-constant demand to go shopping. We need to defend our rights, including the right to have peace and a livable environment, against the demands of the repressors to cede them to the war on terrorism, at least until history offers us a rebirth of excellence in high spiritual and civic places.

May 2002

Those who define "taste" in the highbrow world have eschewed socially relevant themes. Indeed, political and social statements in the art world became quite "tawdry" among the post-World War II artistic elite.

Review of Pollock
(Directed by Ed Harris)

Is it a curse
To review films (about
Paint) in rhyming verse?
In this film about the master
Harris superb as Pollock
never matured you see
He was an alcoholic
Mother didn't accept him
brother went out of town
insight into troubled genius'
very nervous break down
Fortune enters his studio
Did God this woman send?
To love the talented artist
Or a soul to co-depend?
Fifty years of war
And two nuclear bombs
passé to paint faces
while chaotic disaster looms
Critics mocked all substance
Wealthy walls claimed chimera
Rockefeller reacted in horror
To reality ala Rivera
The art world had had it with meaning
Social conscience had gone to the moon
So Pollock with splashes and splotches
Gained fame and then his fortune
But addicts drown in self-pity
can't keep the devil inside
So Pollock ended his story

In murder and then suicide
Did Divinity speak through brushes
That painted a pointless world?
Jackson flicked drops on canvas
As if God's path had unfurled
Did Pollock control his splatter?
Did he intend to appear absurd?
Did his droppings have higher meaning?
Had blemishes replaced His word?
No angels on cathedral ceilings
Nor virgin births to praise
Too many centuries of sin had followed
God's warning to change our ways

March 2001

Advertising Can Make You Personally and Politically Crazy

Welcome to imperial war in the age of the advertising presidency.

When the president boasts that he received "darned good intelligence" about Iraqi weapons of mass destruction and links to Al Qaeda I think he's pushing some new barbecue sauce. What riles me is not just the "lip-smacking good intelligence" or the flagrant photo ops generated by White House staff trained more in publicity than in affairs concerning the common good, but the urgent nature of political messages that emanate from high places.

When Attorney General John Ashcroft or Homeland Security Tsar Tom Ridge warn me about an impending terrorist attack against an airplane or ferry boat, I patiently wait for them to advise me about which product to buy in order to prevent it.

Luckily, I and some of my fellow citizens have constructed mental filters to sift reality from the "emergency" announcements we receive regarding the need to go to war, vote, conserve, spend, relax, exercise, sleep, get energy, and consume the vast variety of goods and services that make up our, and Madonna's, material world. The oft-repeated advertising metaphors invade our consciousness and influence how we deal with needs and wants; the Axis of Evil requires action by the Good. The universal bond of human needs has weakened in the modern era of individualism, which stresses consumption—brand names—*über alles*.

Madison Avenue metaphors dominate current political campaigns and, like the ads about consumer products, they confound public thinking by depriving voters of a proper context for political and personal decisions. Indeed, the PR industry has invented new urges.

We need what we don't want and want what we don't need. For example, we no longer seek "food" when we're hungry. Rather, we need lean cuisine, sushi, Indian delights, or Hunan cooking. Worse, on the downside of our conditioned taste buds we seek grease (not to be confused with the island that provided us with Hellenic culture and delicacies such as stuffed grape leaves and feta cheese) as a source of satisfying not only hunger but a sense of belonging.

Thanks to the massive ad campaign aimed at the car-driving public, especially the ubiquitous billboard signs on highways, we all recognize the golden arches, the colonel, and other commercial logos that have become as familiar to us as the flag and Mickey Mouse. Indeed, according to Eric Schlosser in *Fast Food Nation* (Houghton-Mifflin, 2001), "Americans spend more money on fast food than they do on higher education, personal computers, software, or new cars." One reason for this bizarre spending statistic, Schlosser writes, is the premeditated conditioning of human taste buds.

Schlosser describes the chemical additives industry whose factories near the New Jersey Turnpike produce the tastes that make kids, teenagers, and anxious adults addicted to the sodium and cholesterol-laden fare offered by Burger King, Wendy's, Carl's Jr., and, of course, McDonald's. Indeed, no less a luminary than former President Bill Clinton admitted to his addiction. "I don't necessarily consider McDonald's junk food," Monica's former lover rationalized. "They have chicken sandwiches; they have salads. . . ."

Similarly, we don't cover our bodies to protect us from cold or sun; rather, we wear fashion statements. Those who wear last year's (or last month's) modes or (God forbid) socks with Birkenstocks become the butts of cruel remarks. They lose social status; the fashionably dressed describe them as frumpy or attire-challenged.

Many Americans treat their cars not as a means of travel from point A to point B, but as sex magnets and statements of power and prestige. Cars become objects that take on human attributes. People name their cars as they do pets and talk to them as they screech to a halt during daily freeway mishaps.

TV and print ads assure viewers that "Shell is making waves for cleaner engines," as this polluting company shows a bird flying over ocean waves. This corporation, which has defiled Nature, now advertises as if it were at one with Nature. Or buy the new Ford Destroyer or Dodge Exploder that will enhance sexual prowess as well as increase the amount of honorific deference, which the driver will have mysteriously earned.

Ironically, the advertisers film these motorized instruments of ecological devastation against backdrops of pristine wilderness, as if the SUV, the supreme violation of Nature, actually belongs in an unpopulated arctic reserve. Perhaps, these ads suggest, the owner of a brand-new gas-guzzling road hog should think of himself as an explorer, the first human to reach the untainted beauty of God's creation, thanks to the innate power of the SUV. These virtual polar adventures stand in polar opposition to critical thinking or participating meaningfully in politics.

Advertising appeals to the anxious consumer who has been conditioned to feel inadequate. Instead of encouraging each individual to participate in his or her own history during their short lifetime, the ad-mongers divert us into thinking about our lifetime quests as overcoming individual inadequacies. They set forth norms of perfection as if God had meant all of us to match that undernourished look we see in the TV and magazine models. Instead of the voluptuous beauties who posed for Rubens and other great artists, we get Ally McBeal and the other TV stringbeans that subliminally inform us that the slightest hint of human flesh that doesn't cling tightly to the barest bone signifies ugliness and merits either a crash diet or a rush visit to the liposuction clinic.

Inadequacy of almost any variety can be cured. Feeling wimpy? Lacking a dynamite personality? Buy the "Charisma Chronograph," a watch that not only decorates your wrist but as the name implies, transforms your character, makes you "cool."

Advertisers have successfully propagated the equation of thin and expensive as beautiful and good. They have defined happiness as shopping or taking a shopping vacation. Remember how President W advised the public in the post-September 11 panic to go shopping and take the kids to Disneyland? "Suppose," I ask my students, "everyone would stop buying this season's fashions and stay with the same line year after year; suppose that you ate simple and healthy diets instead of junk food; suppose you demanded public transportation instead of relying on expensive and dangerous cars and SUVs? What would happen?"

To even raise such questions leads one close to penetrating the fragile membrane of the advertising industry. To think critically about daily life might lead us to think about politics as well. To reject the advertising industry's definition of what we need, to reject the consumerist world itself, might well lead to a massive return to the practice of citizenship.

Advertising has elevated the act of shopping to the highest spiritual level while simultaneously diverting us from real politics, that is, playing roles in our own history. Indeed, for fashion the contemporary era relies on the axiom: To shop is in; to be political is out.

Thousands of false messages daily assure the public that they need: more insurance to consolidate their loans, better-smelling soap, more lustrous shampoo, and more teeth-whitening toothpaste, sexier underwear, and sexier cars. Indeed, there is even a "recipe for a simple fulfilling retirement." "Turn to a CERTIFIED PERSONAL PLANNER professional to help you get there." No wonder the "need" to vote pales before the "need" to shop.

Neil Postman called the modern advertising-dominated media phenomenon "amusing ourselves to death," taking off from Aldous Huxley's idea of the diversionist nature of post-modern tyranny in *Brave New World*. Indeed, when critics emerge, the fashion-mongers pelt them with the labels of irrelevance, egotism, and irresponsibility. Ralph Nader, the 2000 Green Party candidate, who attacked the assumptions of corporate nobility, received the label of "dowdy."

Nader's penetrating critique of corporate culture aimed at recruiting citizens, not consumers, to control the corporation and its executives. He described them as everyone now sees them: banal and greedy, not high and mighty.

In the advertising age, democracy should follow the fashions. The writer of the Web-based *Mad Dog* suggests that "Supreme Court Justice Rehnquist post an auction advertising the presidency. Maybe something like: 'Looking for fame, fortune and interns? Become president of the United States. This exclusive position has only been offered 43 times in 227 years and will allow you to join an elite group which includes George Washington, John F. Kennedy, and Millard Fillmore. Generous salary, free housing, world travel, and a good retirement program after as few as four years. Bonus title of Commander in Chief included at no extra cost.' "[2]

August 2002

Commercial Messages Produce
Advanced Scatteration

Like some of my friends and colleagues, I have begun to suffer from "Advanced Scatteration," not to be confused with multitasking, ADD, or dyspepsia. This describes symptoms that occur after listening to and seeing an indeterminate number of important yet incoherent messages that compete for my attention. The result is that I find it difficult to focus on news of the world, nation, and my local region.

Living in Los Angeles, I become even more sated than those in the rest of the country with news that might better wear the label of celebrity tittle-tattle. This chatter about the private lives of the stars commands a serious portion of the news agenda. The star-babble also fills the brain with information that bears no relationship to one's role as citizen, parent, or friend.

For example, after seeing *Entertainment Tonight* just to bond with my teenage daughter, of course, and reading the covers of the scandal mags in the supermarket just to pass the time while waiting to pay for my groceries, I feel that I possess intimate knowledge of Tom Cruise and Nicole Kidman's lives, both during and after their separation and divorce. I've never actually met either of them but, hey, it makes me feel important in a vicarious sort of way to find out from the February 12, 2001, *Divorce Magazine.com* that Tom may have engaged in some hanky-panky with Penelope Cruz and that Nicole, raised Catholic, didn't feel comfortable raising the kids as Scientologists.

This week, I learned that the septuagenarian grandfather of five, Defense Secretary Donald Rumsfeld is more than just a war-mongering hawk. According to the December 2, 2002 *People*, America's most widely read magazine and part of the Time Warner conglomerate, he's the "sexiest Cabinet Member." The article describes Rummy as a man with "that steady gaze, that strong jaw—a man you could trust if all hell were breaking loose."

"That's pretty sexy stuff," continues *People*. This kind of information makes me feel like a virtual insider. I now know that President Bush calls his front man in the war on terror, "Rumstud." Here I am feeling fatuous and inadequate, unable to communicate to those in power the intensity of my feelings against the war with Iraq and I find myself catapulted inside the core of the Washington decision-making circle. Thanks to the gossip magazines and the TV nosy-parkers I can peek into the dressing rooms of power. However, this momentary flight does nothing to help me reason with Rumsfeld the Hunk about his apparent gusto to make war with Iraq. Like most Americans, blitzed by the commercial messages that emphasize our individual shortfalls, I become confused.

I detest Donald Rumsfeld, I say to myself. But that doesn't fit with CNN's image which, according to *People* "dubbed him a 'virtual rock star.'" The slightly rumpled look, the tightly wound expression he wears behind rimless glasses made him a perfect envoy for President Reagan to send to Iraq in 1983 to help Saddam Hussein acquire some of his now unthinkable weapons. Rummy's stern but avuncular demeanor allows him to repeat ad nauseam his charges that Iraq has links to the dreaded Al Qaeda, without feeling obliged to provide a single fact to support his assertion. Indeed, like a B-movie prosecutor he argues that the "absence of evidence is not evidence of absence." Fox News (the word "News" might be an overstatement) called him a Beltway "babe magnet."

"More than any other man in Washington," says Barbara Starr, CNN's Pentagon correspondent, "Don Rumsfeld exercises raw, ruthless power and enjoys it." On the flip side, she adds, Rummy can be "a big flirty pussycat." The ex-Navy pilot is "an old-fashioned, all-American he-man, plain and simple," says Jennifer Harper, media columnist for *The Washington Times*.

After reading the puff piece on a man that previously looked androgynous to me, do I better understand the shortcomings of my sensibility mechanisms? Have I gained more insight from this celebration of the bellicose Rumsfeld than, for example, I did from knowing about a large brown mole on the butt of a famous movie actress or the excruciating details of Rosie O'Donnell's diet? Or even the most detailed information about the kind of food and booze that Snoop Doggy Dogg offers his houseguests?

Sonoma State Professor Peter Phillips and his student researchers Krista Arata and Kathleen O'Rourke-Christopher disparagingly call this phenomenon Junk Food News. In an article in the 2002 *Junk Food News List*,[3] they compiled "a list of the most frivolous over-reported news stories of the year," including "what Gwyneth Paltrow chooses to wear on Oscar night."

Indeed, people know more about the booze arrests of President W and his daughters and his niece Noelle Bush's run-ins with the law and her subsequent foibles at the drug rehab place than they do about the policies of the president or Noelle's father, Florida Governor Jeb Bush. The celebrity "news" that dominates the media contains subliminal messages. These hidden communiqués tend to override the meaning of world and national news. The rich and famous chitchat that masquerades as important information has the effect of putting the rest of us in our place: inadequate and passive voyeurs peeping into the private lives of those who actually *do* things.

The fact that you, the recipient of this gossip called news, do not have sufficient wealth and fame should concern you more than a scandal involving billions of taxpayers' dollars, a sum that is hard to imagine in any case. When the rich and famous talk, they ipso facto convey important messages. Take *Titanic* star Leonardo Di Caprio's response to ABC's Barbara Walters about success and failure.

"I think ultimately success is good," replied Di Caprio. "Failure not so good . . . uh. . . ." Well, Yogi Berra he's not, but ABC-TV executives nevertheless considered the broadcasting of such wisdom quite consistent with their standards for prime-time viewing.

The abysmal level of "standards" relates to the desire of the networks to offer simple "bites" rather than complicated scenarios. Compare the difficulties of understanding the convoluted shenanigans of Enron and WorldCom executives in their theft of billions with the straightforward dalliance of a well-known actress or the routine drug habits of an actor. The stars commit breaches of ethics and morality by screwing the "wrong" people or ingesting "illegal" substances, while the criminal activities of corporate executives, often in collusion with government officials, appear as, yawn, the same old, same old news, remote from even our imaginations.

But some old news bears repeating by the networks. Noncorporate scandals like the 1996 grisly murder of JonBenet Ramsey, the child model, or actor Robert Blake's alleged murder of his wife in 2001, remain a major focus of their Hollywood shows as well as weekly fare for supermarket tabloids. Such gore obviously appeals to the "taste" of millions of Americans. "We give them what we want," the marketers of yellow journalism respond, defending their "gossip as news" approach to the world.

In fact, "they" give us what "they" want in order to sell us what "we" don't need and then claim it is "our" inherent taste "they" are satisfying. Americans receive a heavy conditioning in human nature-altering stimulation from babyhood on. The television and other mass media organs constantly tell them what they should want in order to "fit in," to be "trendy," to appear less inadequate. Junk food news specializes in diverting Americans from participating in their lives as citizens and convinces them that participation means consumption of goods that they want but don't need. Indeed, it conditions them to hate what is good for them and to need what is bad for them: food, for example, becomes anathema to the millions of dieting Americans intent on gaining the undernourished or cut looks (women's liberation has led to two choices) that have become "fashionable."

The profit-making TV world conditions each viewer to think of himself or herself as the center of the universe, the person whose highly individual "tastes" make the mass market function. Given the illusion TV creates of such potential power, it is small wonder that TV advertising then inculcates the notion of personal insufficiency as the viewer's only measure of himself. "What's more important," it asks implicitly, "improving your financial status and appearance or thinking politically?" After decades of such conditioning, I marvel that I had the strength to will myself the energy to vote in a congressional election. The majority of my countrymen and women did not vote. Aside from the glaring similarities in many of the rivals' positions, voting doesn't seem to matter compared to the titillating knowledge available about the "truly important" people and the impending disasters. Daily headlines scream alarms. On November 19, 2002 an Associated Press story started with "Surveillance Expanded After Court Ruling." That day's *Boston Globe* headlined "Ashcroft Gets Unprecedented Powers."

The August 24, 2002 *Washington Post* told of Ashcroft demanding "Record of 17 Senators Probing Sept 11 Attacks." "Historically, Laws Bend in Time of War, Rehnquist Says" states the June 15, 2002 *Los Angeles Times*.

"So, what's any of that got to do with me?" says my teenager's friend.

"What had J.Lo's latest sexcapades, Winona Ryder's 2002 shoplifting conviction, or Puffy's latest clothing design got to do with you?" I ask.

"Hey," says the sixteen-year old. "Those are the in things to know, you know. If you want to belong, I mean." She meant how the "trendy" rags and TV shows define "belonging."

What happened to the hope that essayist E. B. White had for television? He thought it "should be the visual counterpart of the literary essay, should arouse our dreams, satisfy our hunger for beauty, take us on journeys, enable us to participate in events, present great drama and music, explore the sea and sky and the wind and the hills."[4] Or is there too little profit in such a glorious unscattering notion?

December 2002

Television: Democracy at Its Ugliest

"Television," said comedian Fred Allen, "is a triumph of machine over people, and the minds that control it are so small that you could put them in a gnat's navel with room left over for two caraway seeds and an agent's heart."[5]

Like most American parents, I conceded control of my children's minds at certain ages to the perfidious and profit-seeking imaginations of those who program our nation's television stations. Smart as they were, I worried, they would accept as truth the slush they saw on the tube. But I rejected outright coercion as a tactic. My wife sarcastically quoted David Frost, "Television enables you to be entertained in your home by people you wouldn't have in your home."[6]

Despite endless hours of exposure to *The Brady Bunch*, *Three's Company*, *Friends*, and *Seinfeld*, the kids have evolved into conscientious empathetic people. But they did ingest some of television's lessons. How could anyone develop an immune system that could withstand the barrage of messages that dictate all aspects of life and lifestyle? I'm not even referring just to shows like *Jerry Springer* or *Cheaters*, where people eagerly sacrifice their dignity just to appear on television as millions applaud their lack of self-esteem. "I never miss a chance to have sex or appear on television,"[7] Gore Vidal said.

Behind the façade of this "entertainment" medium, a hidden hand has inserted itself. Within the elaborate mechanisms of machines and human hierarchy, television, like all technologies, directs not only personal taste but social life as well. Like the pernicious invisible dictator that hid inside the cute little automobiles of the early twentieth century, the indiscernible imps inside the tube have also become designers of life, organizers of time, and manipulators of space.

Yes, many children still continue to read and participate in public life despite the televised assault on their cognitive apparatus. But who would deny the power of a medium that sixty years ago existed as a sci-fi notion and fifty-five years ago emerged as a silly source of amusement for nitwits? "Television," wrote Ann Landers, "has proved that people will look at anything rather than each other."[8]

Except for the Canadian sociologist Marshall McLuhan (*The Medium Is the Message*), few in the late 1940s and early 1950s predicted that this medium would become an all-encompassing cultural pillar. At that time, clumsy, middle-aged fat men wrestling and Milton Berle's *Texaco Hour* and Sid Caesar's *Show of Shows* dominated the black and white ten-inch screen.

As a teenager in the late 1940s and early 1950s, I watched the box, the tube, the boob tube, the telly, and TV, as it became known. That was before its executives understood the power of their new technology. Perhaps it was the 1954 televised hearings at which Senator Joe McCarthy lost his cool and his dignity in a confrontation with the Secretary of the Army, the whole nation (actually less than ten percent of adults watched it) witnessed the fanatical anti-communist junior Senator from Wisconsin expose himself as a moral buffoon.

At some point in the 1950s television turned from a struggling new media form into a command medium. Now it offers important directives to members of the family from its place in the living room, kitchen, bedroom, and even bathroom. Its silent command, "Turn me on or else," is hard to refuse. This "cool medium," as McLuhan dubbed it because it induces passivity while simultaneously exciting anxiety, became a multipurpose technology. It sold products, amused the masses, and changed the cognitive basis of several generations of people. By invading the realm of basic learning, television created new forms of knowing through its moving images and constantly changing sound track. On the other hand, it weakened traditional sensibilities, and challenged reading and writing for control of the human imagination.

Leading the charge to convert citizens into consumers, television programmers have replaced much of the concern that might have existed for the common good with a focus on the personal as universal. Thanks to the penetration of television into almost every home, Americans share common images, music (jingles), one-liners, and anxieties.

I once thought of life's goal as an ideal combination of love and work. Now, leisure in its idealized TV form substitutes for life. Forget the ads showing people at play, fishing, lounging, and basking in the sun without a mention of melanomas. Think of the TV sitcoms and serials and count the hours where you actually see our heroes working (except for lawyers, doctors, and cops). Leisure rules in the world of *Seinfeld* where some of the characters work from time to time, but where their childless lives revolve around trivia.

Love and work, in the context of family and community, have given way to eternal play, or "playing around" as Monica Lewinsky called her sport, defined on TV as watching other adults play "professional" sports or staring endlessly at changing electronic images from cooking shows to "important" public and educational events to test patterns. Our technology produces wonders by dominating the mysteries of Nature. New machines revolutionize production, usually by reducing the amount of labor involved in a process or figuring out how to extract more labor from the worker. On TV and in the movies the cell phone plays a supporting role. On the street millions of people chat with their lovers, family members, and friends. But think of how the cell phone also allows for the extra utilization of time for salesmen, executives of all levels, and managers. For many workers, what once were leisure hours have turned into work time thanks to those very attractive, if scary on the highway, mobile telephones, laptops, Palm Pilots, and pagers. Often the ads hype them as amusement machines, objects to play with as if they epitomized leisure, the quest of life.

But life requires obedience to the norms of fashion, at which viewers are by definition inadequate. Whether you're over- or underweight, too tall or short, too old or too young, lack body or skin tone, clothes, cars, toys, or the latest gadgets, TV has the prescription: shop and make whatever deficiency you suffer temporarily better.

Television, like the car and computer, has become a force of modern production and life and has etched its methods into the brain. What does this daily barrage of images and sound do to human sensibilities? By placing explicit pictures and exaggerated sound into their cerebral cortexes, it strips people of creativity. Indeed, what does a trip to the shopping mall do? From my own experience both TV and the mall leave me fatigued, irritable, and unsatisfied.

Malls from sea to sea dramatize the notion that shopping represents family spirituality. A day spent traversing the fluorescently lit aisles of chain stores and fast food outlets in search of "bargains" may erode sensibilities and destroy creativity, but it does leave the shoppers anxious and tired. Masses, as the marketers think of people, will focus on their personal problems, as sensory overload and stress increase, and seek medication through purchases of more commodities. This nullifies any possibility of thinking about public affairs, let alone listening to or engaging in meaningful discourse.

Television has also altered the nature of leisure. Americans once applied their skills as artisans, they read and then discussed, even by correspondence, with others who shared the same literary experience. We learned from grade school through university that Americans historically made decisions through voting based on ideas of the public good. But we didn't learn back in the 1940s and 1950s that our real daily and weekly decisions would involve brand names and fashions.

I watch my teenager thumb through *Seventeen* and *YM*. I surreptitiously filch them for quick bathroom reads to discover that the publishers of these teen magazines fill their pages with anxiety-producing stories about weight, acne, and looming failure with boys. The girl whose skin is not perfect, who possesses an extra ounce in the "wrong place," should feel the fears of imminent malfunction. Boys will shun her! These teen magazines reproduce themselves on TV.

TV executives ordered writers and producers to design versions of some mainstream magazines like *People* and *Cosmopolitan* for the "teenage market." Shows such as *Beverly Hills 90210* and *Melrose Place* have evolved into product-pushing "teen-friendly" serials such as *Dawson's Creek*, *Buffy the Vampire Slayer* (featuring a slightly curved toothpick who slays sexy vampires), and *Charmed*, which shows that "female empowerment" derives from well-coiffed girls having cute but very bare midriffs, the clues to possessing special powers. Each girl can and should aspire to such heights, says the subliminal message.

In China, India, Indonesia, and much of the third world, how could an individual conceive of herself as the center of the world, alone fighting the competition for boys, status, prestige, and honorific deference? The masses of the third world receive daily doses of consumption assumptions. The reality of their lives, however, removes them from the possibility of even tasting the sweet-sour essence of modern middle-class America. But the superimposition of media aesthetics often leads them to reject or at least question their traditional roots.

Television promotes individualism in a mass-market world. It elevates leisure to the level of a life goal. One works to gain money to afford leisure. One uses the money to buy things that will bring individual and family happiness. This weapon of mass distraction tries to confuse us by equating individuality with individualism. Luckily several billion people still understand that they are not what they wear. They have not yet imbibed the pervasive distortion of philosophy offered by this once cool, but now tepid medium: "I shop therefore I am."

November 2002

Clear Channel Fogs the Airwaves

Swiss novelist Max Frisch described technology as "the knack of so arranging a world that we need not experience it."[9] Since Frisch died in 1991, just before the "information age" reached its commercial maturity, he missed some zany interpretations of his wisdom. Greg Collins, a senior vice president of Reynolds and Reynolds Company, offers his understanding of Frisch in *Ward's Dealer Business*, February 1, 2003.

"Unfortunately," Collins laments, "many businesses still approach technology from the 'Industrial Age' mentality of days past." Collins' future orientation refers to businessmen using technology to improve business processes, not just to reduce their labor force. "Once the truth is known, it's remarkable how effective people, processes and technology can be" at enhancing corporate profits. Frisch turns uneasily in his grave.

Truth and corporate profits go together like Tabasco sauce on vanilla ice cream. Indeed, modern corporations gain from massive fabrication about the products they peddle just as media giants make money from lying on the hourly "news" reports they scream at the public. Indeed, audiences have become accustomed to listening to lies masquerading as truth. Each day thousands of commercial, political, and religious "messages" pour over the TV and radio waves, all designed to make us do or buy something we don't need to do or buy.

I shake my head in confusion just from living in this mother of all information ages. If I read, watch TV, look at highway billboards, or turn my radio dial from classical music to "all news when it happens," I receive machine gun blasts of mis- and dis-information, manipulative words, pictures, (spam) sounds, and symbols aimed at converting my organism into an advanced purchasing instrument. No one has yet invented the equivalent of the bulletproof vest for the brain, to protect against the cartridges of blather fired at our cerebral cortex.

I assume advertisers and news fabricators (those who invent the lies and those who report them) count on rapid temporal atrophy among the receivers of their false information. I can actually feel my brain filter growing overtaxed with bullpucky: terrorism, orange alerts, snipers, SARS! Who said what, when, where? Huh? How much of my pension did I lose in the market today? Will I still have my job when I get to work? The messages of anxiety penetrate beyond any "facts."

A man with a baritone voice claims to know Jesus Christ personally. "Give Jesus Christ a chance," he exhorts his listeners. He wants all of us to experience the born-again Christian rapture like the Republican who occupies the White House.

The radio missionary sounds serious. The radio station owners are very serious—about undertaking the Lord's work and simultaneously seeking ever greater profits (market shares). Take the Clear Channel radio stations. On the air, they offer dumbed-down religiously tinged versions of reality. Off the air, in their corporate boardrooms, the media executives engage in sophisticated business practices. The hard-rock material foundations for broadcasting church sermons come replete with off-the-air business conspiracies. On the air: Simplify life for the listeners. Turn to Jesus! Vote Republican! Wave the flag!

Clear Channel literally fogs the airwaves with ultra-right slogans that appeal to the fundamentalist white Christian soldiers of God. Now, shudder, Clear Channel plans to capture the Spanish-speaking radio audience as well. They await only a tiny change of rules by the Federal Communications Commission (FCC).[10]

When the FCC approves its nearly $2.5 billion deal, according to Eric Boehlert in the April 24, 2003 *Salon*, Clear Channel would link the Hispanic Broadcasting Corporation of which it owns 26 percent, "the leader in Spanish-language radio stations in the U.S. with Univision Communications—already the market leader in Spanish-language TV, cable and music." This new entity "would create a new company that controls nearly 70 percent of Spanish-language advertising revenue in the United States."

Univision uses formula programming, flag-waving news, and public affairs shows, stale music templates remixed with electronic technology, and very loud commercials. Put together two financial powerhouses in their world of programming mediocrity and you have an ideal vehicle for messianic Republican propaganda.

Boehlart recalls that "President Bush even gave Univision his first national television interview following his inauguration. More recently, congressional Democrats have grumbled over Univision's fawning coverage of Miguel Estrada, the conservative—and controversial—judge recently nominated by Bush to serve on the U.S. Court of Appeals."

Clear Channel stations openly advocate for Republican causes. Indeed, one Democratic member of Congress recently accused Clear Channel of blatantly skewing its war coverage to favor the administration. Like the bombastic Rush Limbaugh of the EIB media conglomerate, Clear Channel has no apologies. Its executives proudly stand for the values of George W. Bush.

But while Clear Channel talk-show hosts and preachers piously pound away at "family values," the corporate executives practice their shark-like business plans. Family values in the media business mean the FCC will validate corporate media mergers. The new rules would tighten the already strong hold that the five monster conglomerates have over TV and radio networks.

Clear Channel executives expect the FCC to reinterpret the "public interest" to mean a near-monopoly over TV and radio for their stations along with their ideological pal Rupert Murdoch's Fox network, the electronic and defense titan General Electric, and the CNN patriots. Imagine these sources as the "information" providers for the majority of Americans. Boehlart says Clear Channel "took advantage of the Tele-communications Act of 1996" to grow from "40 stations then to approximately 1200 stations today, or roughly 970 more than its closest competitor."

If you're frightened by these figures, you've reacted correctly. While liberals and progressives debate morality and justice, the extreme right-wing media moguls muscularly push their simplistic nativism on the TV and radio waves and seek ever more space to reach out with their revealed word sandwiched, of course, between commercial messages so that ever more Americans will get the messianic virus. Politically, Clear Channel and Univision represent the neoconservative-fundamentalist Christian worldview in both the ideological and business sense.

Their power extends beyond politics, however. In Latin music, Univision or Clear Channel can promote "their hits" on "their stations." According to Boehlart, Clear Channel also owns "37 television stations, 770,000 billboards and unmatched lists of venues, promoters and tours to exert control over the concert industry. Last year the company sold 30 million concert tickets, or 26 million more than its closest competitor."

With this kind of material power, Clear Channel can unleash its ideological pit bulls on the air. Talk show host Glenn Beck sponsored "Rallies for America" as Bush sought signs of public backing for his impending war to counter antiwar rallies that had successfully received some news coverage. Clear Channel not only acted as impresario for the pro-war demonstrations, but heavily promoted these boring events on its radio stations.

Boehlart reports that with Clear Channel approval one Denver disc jockey "suggested that then antiwar Vermont Governor Dean should be shot. Musicians got the political message Clear Channel was sending. During a speech at the National Press Club last week, actor and outspoken antiwar activist Tim Robbins told reporters, "A famous middle-aged rock-and-roller called me last week to thank me for speaking out against the war, only to go on to tell me that he could not speak himself because he fears repercussions from Clear Channel. 'They promote our concert appearances,' he said. 'They own most of the stations that play our music. I can't come out against this war.'"

Can watching TV produced by such intimidators lead to creativity? Watching for a few hours, I concluded that my undergraduate students make more interesting telenovelas than the Spanish language soaps on Univision. The programming that Latinos receive and what they will get in the near future as Clear Channel and Univision perform their kinky business marriage may make the *Jerry Springer Show* and *Cheaters* seem highly intellectual.

Highbrows may sneer at TV in general or claim that they watch only PBS, yawn, but this will not defeat the tasteless and "friendly fascism" (as Bertram Gross called it in his 1982 book by that name) of our age. Media moguls have used technology to arrange values to suit their commercial proclivities: want what you don't need; need what you don't want; salute and wave the flag and give what's left of your mind to Jesus and George W. Bush. Yes, Max Frisch died before technology had rearranged the media world so as to vitiate experience.

Revised: July 2003

The Film Industry: Business and Ideology

Through the movies, a Frenchman remarked, the United States
has effected the 'cultural colonization' of the world.
—Leo Rosten

The US motion picture industry, like other entertainment businesses, works with government to make a profit and culturally colonize the rest of the world. "In the mid-1960s," according to Tyler Cohen, in the April 28, 2003 *Forbes.com*, "American films accounted for 35 percent of box office revenues in Continental Europe; today the figure is between 80 percent and 90 percent." Why would sophisticated Europeans and devout Buddhists pay money to see films like *Dumb and Dumber*?"

Cohen concludes that "Hollywood films . . . are technically advanced (e.g., special effects) and heavily advertised and publicized in the mass media. The typical European film has about 1 percent of the audience of the typical Hollywood film, and this differential has been growing. American movies have become increasingly popular in international markets, while European movies have become less so."

European films, slower in pace, appear to hyperactive US audiences as unbearably heavy tomes filled with ideas, philosophical comments, and nuanced relationships. And, as Cohen points out, "the training of cinematic talent in the US and Europe reflects these differences. American film schools are like business schools in many regards."

Compare the best US film schools (UCLA, NYU, or USC as examples) with the cinema program at the University of Krakow in the 1950s that turned out directors such as Roman Polanski and Andres Wajda. Instead of training for a job in the industry, the Polish curriculum emphasized liberal arts and humanities. Actual training for lighting, camera operation, acoustics, and the like, took place in the last year of a five-year program. US film schools "train" rather than "educate" from the beginning. They hold out promises that right after graduation, their trainees can become assistant editors or associate producers, defined by Fred Allen as "the only person who would associate with a producer."[11]

From its inception in the early twentieth century, business grammar captured American cinema. Entrepreneurs devised formulas to transform a new "art form" into commodities that would attract large, poorly educated audiences likely to return next week for more captivating celluloid mind fodder. Over the decades, technological perfection came to substitute for the innovative dynamic of artistic creation. Indeed, the industry built its worldwide reputation on Hollywood craftsmen's ability to simulate reality. It challenged all foreign rivals and independents to match it. Hollywood elevated the perfection of animation and special effects technology, for example, into the criteria on which mass media critics should pass their first judgment on films. Anything less than its standard of technical excellence would amount to the equivalent of offering a new car with an ugly scratch on the paint job. Trace the industry from the silent but technologically advanced racist epic, *Birth of a Nation* to the twenty-first century musicals *Moulin Rouge* or *Chicago*. Technology as art wins audiences.

Aesthetic judgments aside, each Hollywood movie required, first and foremost, a business plan. To pass on a film idea, studio executives fashioned a profit-making blueprint, "Give us scripts," they ordered the writers, "that will lure audiences to theaters and keep them coming back." This success formula spun off candy, popcorn, and soft drink profits as well as Hollywood itself as a special culture from which countless other industries developed. Naturally, for the first six decades of the industry, the producing studios also owned the movie theaters.

Hollywood studios helped create audiences by offering what Irwin Shaw called "the American dream made visible," which included cultivating the star system. Behind the powerless but rich glamorpusses and dashing heroes of the silent screen, sat the multimillionaire studio moguls who manipulated "the talent."

Using simplistic recipes produced by the writers, defined by studio boss Jack Warner as "schmucks with Underwoods," and the technology of the giant screen, movies conditioned excitement-starved audiences to expect magical Saturday afternoons and evenings.

By the twenty-first century, virtual technology had rescued once-challenged filmmakers from actually finding locations and figuring out how to actually render them credible through the filming and editing processes. Software and digital technology now "render" the drama of a precipitous gorge or lush jungle. Technology has enhanced the industry's possibilities for commercially designing and manufacturing cinema magic. It has not improved the idea quality. Indeed, few expect such "highbrow" offerings.

Buying a ticket means that one leaves credibility at the box office along with the price of admission. The lights fade and impossibly beautiful people appear. They don't die in high-speed chases or falls from insufferable heights.

In addition, publicity and the 24/7 nature of contemporary TV and the Web have extended Hollywood's trivia to cognitive proportions. On TV and in supermarket tabloids, actors' personal lives take on vicarious energy. They substitute for excitement in one's own life. The untold numbers of shows, articles, and Web shorts deal exclusively with the dalliances of the stars. The people we stare at sympathetically in films, who shoot with amazing accuracy, make perfect love every time (to romantic music, of course), and rarely deal with children, poverty, or the banality of everyday routine, show off their wardrobes, cleavages, houses, furniture, and pools—and their attention deficit disorders for all things except attention.

We "escape" to the movies to watch emaciated models with baby-smooth skin do and wear things we don't or can't. Then we learn "the shocking truth." Kim Basinger, who I drooled over as the beautiful hooker in *LA Confidential*, is really shy. Her steady relationship with Alec Baldwin dissolved because she abhorred life on Long Island, where he felt at home. Gossip unfurls, intercut with film clips of Kim, now in her late forties and looking thirty. The narrator pauses over a Hollywood mug shot, another episode in the fictionalized lives of truncated people far from the monotony of our jobs, boring school, or tedious house and child care.

Behind the glitter, the film industry produces its commodities for two reasons: profit and reproduction. The motion picture industry resembles the automobile industry: big and shiny-looking products on the outside. But don't look under the hood, or on the cutting-room floor. Both industries rely on beauty and spectacular landscape to sell products.

The commercial world lures the public into the virtual setting, the theater where the available light shines on the screen, where a face (after hours in the makeup room and years spent with "beauty experts") appeals to you to love it, sympathize with it, fear for it. "An emotional Detroit," actress Lillian Gish called Hollywood.

Hollywood's marketing success begins with the assumption that youth and undernourishment constitute universal aesthetics. My teenager takes these criteria seriously and thus refuses to accompany us to the movies. She doesn't want to be seen in public with us, and we find her tastes at the local outlets less than appetizing. In July 2003, we have sequels to *Charlie's Angels*, *The Matrix*, *Legally Blonde 2*, and *The Terminator*.

In these films actors run "the gamut of emotions from A to B," as the late Dorothy Parker put it.

"Why," I ask my daughter, "do gossip shows about movie stars or pop singers excite you?"

"Get real!" she responds.

I deduce that since I'm no longer young enough to know everything, I should recall how teenagers went nuts over skinny Frank Sinatra in the '40s, before the undernourished crooner turned into a national idol, another product of the star system.

"Romantic hoopla," as Leo Rosten calls "Hollywood's amorous acrobatics," became highly profitable on the one hand and diversionary on the other. It can market anything. For example, take the rare film personality who fights for justice. Hollywood presents millionaire Julia Roberts as Erin Brockovich versus the polluting gas and electric company, as the woman with whom the oppressed can identify. Occasionally, a producer sneaks through a socially relevant film that eschews the shoot 'em up, beat 'em up or screw 'em up formula. These films can indeed inspire some people to emulate the fictional characters. Compare them in number to films that teach audiences to identify with their oppressors: good cops, wise bankers, trustworthy governors, or sympathetic Mafia dons.

Such exceptional films prove the rule. Hollywood is a worldwide business whose product includes "American values," from the John Wayne pseudo-macho notion of obeying patriotic orders to the notion that no amount of clothes suffices, as Reese Witherspoon goes through endless costuming in her *Legally Blond* roles.

Beneath thin plot and story lines, embellished by skilled photography, special effects, set design, costuming, makeup, mood music scoring, and the variety of photography tricks employed, one finds a world designed to divert—entertain—at the lowest common denominator.

The Hollywood sales manager instructs his team to "take this crap and sell it to the world as the greatest art and entertainment ever made." God Bless America, especially the one that Hollywood invented!

July 2003

4

Ahab Can Beat the Whale

I don't like nature. It's big plants eating little plants, small
fish being eaten by big fish, big animals eating each other . . .
it's like an enormous restaurant.
—Woody Allen, *Love and Death*

At Two with Nature

I awake when my combination alarm clock/computer-driven coffeemaker kicks in. As the sounds of Beethoven flirt sensuously with the aroma of my organic Chiapas blend (originating from a cooperative and marketed by some group connected to the politically correct Working Assets) drifting through the house, I consult my Palm Pilot for my agenda, check the three-hundred-plus new e-mails and surf the Web (the DSL line means no waiting) for possible excitement from Kazakhstan, while my mechanical toothbrush stimulates my gums.

Online, electronic and digital images provide me with "news" of the world, including weather. In between flash reports from remote places, commercials appear. My eyes have accustomed themselves to filter out several thousand unwanted messages a day.

My microwave oven intones distressingly, reminding me that its electronic timer has determined that I should remove my instant oatmeal. I check that the pulse on the nightlight sensor has deactivated itself along with the all-night electronic and sensor detection devices. The automatic garage door still responds to my own private two-set command that invariably sends its mysterious machinery into action.

Thoreau said that "men have become tools of their tools."[1] Surely, he could not have meant the kind of lifestyle we lead! I think about my several coast-to-coast drives on the superhighway. Yes, one can traverse the United States without seeing it. Or fly over it and get the overview! Thoreau once thanked God that "men cannot yet fly and lay waste to the sky as well as the earth."[2] Hey, even through the daily emissions of tens of thousands of passenger and military jets the spy satellites' cameras can still see well enough on earth to pinpoint a pimple on a teenager's chin. Has technology conquered Nature? If so, what to think about Albert Einstein's remark, "Technological progress is like an axe in the hands of a pathological criminal."[3]

For centuries, natural law or the laws of Nature allowed man to attain the true and the good, which could be accessed through the beautiful. So, the pristine landscape, the purity in the sound of a Mozart refrain, or a young girl wistfully playing in a garden symbolized both beauty and truth.

From the Greeks onward, images and sounds forged organically with Nature became the artistic and philosophical standard. Aristotle based his aesthetics on the link between the beautiful and the good.

It took Tolstoy, a Russian noble who lived until 1910, describing the life of poor peasants to understand that identification of beauty with goodness is illusion. Aside from how current fashion magazine editors manipulate the very essence of beauty from season to season (sometimes less than four months long), some readers have begun to understand the cultural basis of beauty and therefore of good as well. Except for the modern industrial high-tech world, beauty and good link to the land, to Nature untouched. Indeed, traditionally peasants pray before breaking the earth and often weep after disturbing their "mother," the soil.

I try to imagine George W. Bush even considering the implications to Nature after he orders more clearing of forests for the benefit of the multinational tree choppers, more drilling in the pristine wilderness for the global oil barons, and more "development" in hitherto "preserved" sanctuaries.

Infrequently, I still yearn to feel myself inside a truly natural setting. I take up the challenge and walk out into the world. I suppress the urge to take a deep breath when I note that at 7 AM, the smog has already colored the clouds a combination dirty brown-orange and my nose twitches from the unnatural stench emitted by half-a-million dairy cows from nearby Chino.

A teenager in a $50 thousand-plus Hummer hums by spewing fumes and noise. He wears a grin that bespeaks both pride and love of his vehicle, symbolic power. Angelenos love their cars. JD Salinger, that retrograde novelist, wrote that he preferred a horse to a car because "at least a horse is human, for God's sake."

Next to the tree trimmers performing their annual chainsaw slashing of live oaks and mulberries, the Mexican gardeners wield their mowing machines, edgers, and leaf-blowers to create what has become a natural racket, like a herd of crickets with 50 horsepower legs. A teenager on his way to school zooms past on a very loud motorized scooter. I used one of those as I child, except I propelled it with my foot.

I look upward for serenity and try to invoke in myself a state of awe and wonder at my natural—well, sort of—surroundings, or what's left of them. I ask myself, "What relationship do I have with the majestic, snow-capped Mt. Baldy?" I hear no answer from above. Maybe I could travel south or west to the mighty Pacific Ocean, which continues to roll its waves onto the shores of the slowly eroding beaches. The surfers still find some sense of identity there. Of course, just sixty miles to the east lies the desert, where casinos and retirement communities with attached golf courses and country clubs blossom in the culturally dry sand.

Some of my friends seek connection with Nature through bird watching; others dive deep to watch brightly colored fish swim among sharks. They even take photos of these specimens to show those of us who prefer the surface some of the wonders that lie beneath. Millions take nature hikes or walks through botanical or zoological gardens.

The choice, if this word makes any sense, to dominate the natural world for the purpose of progress through the vehicle of science has led to an amazing array of technological "breakthroughs." Simultaneously, it has placed humans in peril against a Nature that appears to have begun rebelling against our excesses. Our way of life, made possible by the very science that brought us plastic, also produced immense contamination. The shining metal surfaces that we expect from new cars and other appliances require heavy solvents to bring out that "clean" look. Chlorines and bromines, the perfect cleansers, also toxify the atmosphere. For decades, the residues from manufacturing plastic and cleaning metals have found their way into rivers, the community's breathing air, and into the soil. Finally, these stories found their way into the media. Panic ensued, followed by a gradual acceptance of the ubiquitous "pollution problem."

By the 1970s, newspaper editors already began yawning when young reporters brought them yet another story about pollution in the Hudson or Mississippi Rivers. Andrew Malcolm observed that "rivers in the United States are so polluted that acid rain makes them cleaner."[4] Such sarcasm underlines the fact that we have come to accept the destruction of Nature as routine.

Does this mean that people now eschew possibilities of regaining true organic connections and accept the vicarious brushes and the virtual touches with Nature as sufficient? After all, society's leaders celebrate as the basis of our civilization the technology that alienates us from the natural world. And in less than a century, technology-based civilization has marched forward with seven-league boots. As Will Rogers put it, "You can't say civilization don't advance. In every war they kill you in a new way."[5]

Our world has outstripped even the sci-fi imaginations of the past. In the eighteenth and nineteenth centuries, who could have imagined nuclear weapons? For Goethe's Faust fulfillment derives not from the selfish quest for pure self-realization but rather from the simple acceptance of the eternal human condition. Faust strives for more, knowledge to realize the secret of Nature, God's secret. He cuts the proverbial deal with the Devil and learns the evil of his ways. Faust then undergoes the redemption process, which entails for him the heaviest of prices, torturous blindness. He saves his soul before death takes him.

The romantic poets and essayists who absorbed Goethe idealized Nature from their urban settings. "If eyes were meant for seeing," wrote Ralph Waldo Emerson in "The Rhodara," "then beauty is its own excuse for being."[6] Fifty years ago a few conservationists and naturalists tried to shout warnings that serious peril lay ahead for the future of Nature's beauty, but few heard them. Rachel Carson's works stand out as exemplary for being ahead of her time.

In poetry classes, students enjoyed Wordsworth's line, "I am at one with nature," empathizing with him as he walked through his nineteenth-century garden. The next century brought out the contradictions. The automobile turned snow into something else. "I'm as pure as the driven slush,"[7] remarked Tallulah Bankhead one winter. "Horsepower," some wit once quipped, "was a truly wonderful thing when only horses had it." Imagine if horsepower could feel frustration as it sits contained in the idling engine of a commuting car on a clogged Los Angeles freeway! And when motorists exercise the horsepower the scientists have congealed into the engine of a car, we invariably get speeding tickets, or worse, have fatal accidents.

By the late twentieth century the kind of organic sentiments expressed by romantic poets seemed impossible to realize. "I am two with Nature," snapped Woody Allen, the quintessence of a city boy. He also summed up the post-existential mood of the developed world. "More than any time in history mankind faces a crossroads. One path leads to despair and utter hopelessness, the other to total extinction. Let us pray that we have the wisdom to choose correctly."[8]

Compare the romantics with Woody's twentieth-century vision. Imagining a new play, he fantasized, "The curtain rises on a vast primitive wasteland, not unlike certain parts of New Jersey."[9] The stench when driving past Secaucus on the New Jersey Turnpike provides an antidote to whimsies about our relationship to some unspoiled natural setting. In an unplanned and often criminal conspiracy, small groups of people around the world have destroyed the very creation they celebrate at church: God's gift to mankind.

Just as Faust aspired to understand the secret of and then conquer Nature, so did Marx who saw such progress as a positive outcome of developing science. In the twentieth century, man (a few of us anyway) has not only conquered large hunks of Nature and submitted them to his promiscuous will, but he has induced Nature to rebel, fight back and symbolically inflict global warming patterns, depleted ozone layers, and other phenomena that "challenge" science.

Goethe's Faust is a far cry from the contemporary Fausts who in 1945 conquered the atomic secret, provided the ignorant generals with that power to destroy Nature, and watched it tested on two Japanese cities.

Crisis mentality led to the production of atomic weapons. But some of the scientists who made Fat Man and Little Boy, as they jocularly named their two A-bombs, did it to defeat Hitler's monstrous plan; others fantasized about the peaceful uses of atomic energy as if somehow the other "problems" associated with nuclear power would disappear.

After the obliteration in the post-World War II period of several Pacific islands used for "testing" the weapons, the scientists observed how cancers spread throughout the test region, and the contamination extended to land, water, air, and animals. Finally, the military, now in charge of the soulless Fausts, had to stop their "scientific" play when the public got panicked and forced the nuclear thugs to test underground.

But even now, some sixty years after the first test at Alamagordo, New Mexico, Nature responds to the punishment it received. On November 23, 2002, the *New Mexican* reported that "Los Alamos County and U.S. Forest Service personnel who are thinning trees in Bayo Canyon east of Los Alamos have been warned by Los Alamos National Laboratory not to remove trees they cut in various parts of the canyon because the trees might be radioactive." According to reporter Wes Smalling, sections of Bayo Canyon, a popular hiking and horseback riding spot, "were used from the 1940s until 1961 as test sites by scientists studying explosions."

LANL spokesman James Rickman admitted that the Atomic Energy Commission conducted tests "at the site called the RaLa Experiments," and that they "involved radioactive lanthanum." But, Rickman assures the reporter, the thinning was stopped "not because it presents any reasonable risk. It's just a precaution."

Huh? If there's no reasonable risk then there's no reason to take precautions.

Rickman digs his own hole deeper. "There's a negligible amount of trees in those areas anyway. But, nevertheless, we wanted to point that out in those areas."

Rickman confesses that "impurities in the lanthanum also produced small amounts of Strontium 90, a radioactive material prevalent in nuclear fallout that has a half-life of 28 years." In other words, if you breathe it, drink it, or eat it, "it would tend to appear in your bones and teeth."

If you want to panic, read the last sentence. "The thinning project has an added importance now because of the contaminants," the story said. Erosion and flooding are likely to occur if an intense forest fire burns in the canyon. The water could carry hazardous material toward homes in Los Alamos," Rickman said.

This kind of story routinely appears. Mercury in fish, high levels of cancerous pesticide in fruits and vegetables, dubious hormones and antibiotics fed to livestock, and, of course, the recent outbreaks of mad cow disease, *e. coli*, and other deadly infirmities, all from science applied to our food intake.

Scientists regularly conduct "experiments" without thinking about consequences, other than profits for the company that employs them. In the Los Alamos case "national security" provided the urgency factor, as it did when other scientists decided from the mid-1940s through the early 1970s to dump hot nuclear waste into the Atlantic and Pacific Oceans. In other words, two factors, commercial gain and "national security" induced scientists to defy the laws of Nature, indeed, the wisdom of millennia.

So, the acceleration of the destruction of Nature occurs under the duress of laws of capital and reasons of State.

No reason not to set my alarm/computer-driven coffeemaker for tomorrow!

December 2002

Commuting in Los Angeles

Time screams profane words
In muffled engine bellows
During long freeway drives
God paints His images
In cracked blistered concrete
Mobiles with moving cars
Teach lessons in physics
This must have meaning
I comfort my worried
Mind with such platitudes
Unwilling to truly accept
That I ride upon
The fragile top soil
Separating me from Hell
Or some un-landscaped place

October 2002

Privatize—The Key to Public Culture

Having survived the first anniversary of 9/11 without suffering another massive attack, the White House sent forth its reassuring interpretation, "We do live in the best of all possible worlds. We come closest to representing what God had in mind when He offered us a chance for redemption."

Indeed, President Bush, with religious zeal characteristic of alcoholics who convert to Christian fundamentalism without passing through AA, eagerly extols Americans to export our way of life to those who haven't yet tasted its spiritual rewards, especially those numerous residents of China, India, and Brazil, "the big markets" as we now know them. Should they do as we say, they too will experience "progress."

For W, privatization has become the key to forging ahead in the world of corporate globalization. Leaders of the industrialized world lectured third-world peoples on this virtue at the UN Conference on Sustainable Development in Johannesburg, South Africa, August 26 to September 4, 2002. Bush dispatched Secretary of State Colin Powell (W had more pressing issues on his ranch) for only the last two days of the summit to admonish African nations against making resources and land public. Meanwhile, some third-world leaders openly worried about their people's lack of access to water, recently privatized in Bolivia.

Privatization became a political axiom during the Reagan era. With his mantra of "love the wonderful corporation," he taught Americans to hate their government (except for the wonderful military establishment, of course) and resist paying taxes to it. CEOs embody the virtues of vision and efficiency and can do better things with your money than government, the former actor intoned. What would you rather have: a good school for your kids or an expensive yacht for a corporate CEO and his friends?

The choice is clear, you say? Well, go back to Reagan. Instead of "taxing and spending," the charge Republicans made against Democrats, Reagan just spent. Reagan rewarded the already rewarded and convinced a majority of voters that it served their own interest to vote against themselves. As the rich became measurably richer, Reagan took advantage of a historic antipathy that poorer citizens have felt toward their government since the American Revolution.

Ironically, instead of shrinking the total government, Reagan enlarged the least productive sectors, while reducing the most important ones. He downsized those agencies that helped people with education, health, and other services and enlarged the military budget by developing sci-fi antimissile programs and redundant missile systems designed to fight the Soviet enemy that was about to collapse under its own weight.

So, two decades later, when serious systemic problems arose at home—health care, energy, and transportation inside an ailing economy—the new president used the illogical but politically tested axioms of free-market ideology to solve them. Privatize the problem, meaning sell public property on the cheap or use government funds to reward corporate campaign contributors in the name of solving a crisis. For example, Bush promoted Enron's deregulation demands which Enron executives manipulated to bilk Californians out of billions of dollars during the 2001 energy crisis.

Because corporations back in the 1920s and afterwards successfully pushed for the destruction of public transportation, the car and the freeway became California's answer to moving from one place to another. Now, from Los Angeles to the San Francisco Bay Area, as far south as suburban San Jose, and from Los Angeles south one hundred miles to San Diego, transportation has become a nightmare that intrudes into other areas of urban life. Poor air quality prevails in highly populated areas despite rigid emission controls. Freeways push their way into urban space and simultaneously grow more clogged, even on weekends. When faced with these issues, corporate and government masterminds concluded that instead of building public transportation, taxpayers should finance yet more freeways, which will lead to vastly increased numbers of cars on the road.

The new freeway after all will facilitate automobile commuters' journeys in their seventy-mile trek from mushrooming bedroom communities east of San Bernardino into downtown Los Angeles or other urban centers. Tens of thousands of three- and four-bedroom units, as houses are now called, have been built or are under construction in the bedroom and shopping mall communities east of LA.

What're a few hundred thousand more people in an area that already contains some tewlve million! So what if the region has a dubious supply of water, mostly stolen, or borrowed, from other regions, never to be paid back of course! Big deal that Californians had a few rolling blackouts! "Development," as construction of freeways, housing clusters, malls, and parking lots is euphemistically known, pushes ever onward.

The great radio philosopher, Rush Limbaugh, believes public transportation smacks of socialism. Indeed, Southern Californians seem to support his thesis. They have learned to love their cars and tolerate torturous conditions daily to maintain their individual means of transportation, if not their closest friend.

A 2002 study in the *Los Angeles Times* showed that LA commuters averaged fifty-six hours last year sitting immobile, not even inching along, on our world-famous freeways. Residents of other car-loving cities spent a few hours less in these situations. This is institutionalized loneliness. Imagine spending the equivalent of two entire days plus one full working shift sitting on a freeway, exhaust fumes pouring out of thousands of vehicles and seeping into your car!

Indeed, Limbaugh and his fellow sages offer freeways and cars as God's way to meet transportation needs. They also say they know that drilling for oil in the Alaska wilderness is the Lord's solution to the energy crisis. President Bush announced that drilling for oil off shore and in the virgin territories equals patriotism. If God hadn't wanted us to drill in those remote Alaskan preserves, why would he have put the oil there in the first place, intimates Limbaugh. Since we export and import almost everything else, why not import more oil? Let's not even talk about semi-socialist endeavors such as wind and solar power or other nonfossil fuel energy sources.

So, W plans to solve the economic and energy crisis by lowering taxes for the rich and drilling for oil and gas in virgin areas. And, presumably, he will help diffuse the transportation crisis by encouraging Congress to spend ever more money building freeways to accommodate ever more cars, many of which we might export to third-world nations so they too can have this kind of progress.

The idea that growth equals development has also become an axiom. Our system assumes that each individual should have the ability to buy as many cars, houses, and boats as he or she pleases, regardless of race, color, or creed. Eventually, the Chinese, Indians, and Brazilians will also learn these lessons as they adopt our way of life. Then they too can live in the best of all possible worlds.

The ruling Chinese communists have adopted pieces of the consumer-producer model and have privatized portions of what had been public property. As proof of China's standing inside the world of global trade, note her entrance into the World Trade Organization with White House support.

In his ardor to promote unfettered access for US capital throughout the world, Bush successfully demanded that Congress vote for "fast track," which the White House equated with patriotism and standing with the prez on the war against terrorism. In reality, fast track is a euphemism for a banal scheme that allows the president to negotiate trade deals without Congress debating them. Congress gets only a yes or no vote on each contract.

For their own Muslim fascist reasons Al Qaeda opposes the western way of life. Ironically, their violent attacks against the symbols of the "progress order" have made it easier for Bush and company to obscure the crisis issues of the prevailing economic model, ones that confront citizens daily on the congested freeways. The commuters cough from the poor air and worry about being late for work, picking up the kids, or seeing the family.

This doesn't mean, however, that citizens must ignore the obvious. As Bush calls for attention to the war on terrorism, don't forget other values, ones that allow for maximum freedom and do not coincide with elevating shopping and SUV driving to the highest spiritual plateau.

September 2002

Will the Next War Be Against Smog?

Freeway driving produces smog anxiety. How much noxious air can I inhale before my lungs give way to emphysema, pneumonia, or some form of chronic cough? I feel my nasal passages twinge, the precursor to a full-fledged sinus rebellion. My nose leaks. I look at my eyes in the rearview mirror, now blazing red, almost crimson. In minutes they will start dripping goop down my cheeks and nose.

Switching radio stations, one of my methods to divert attention from my own physical and mental misery, has proven less than satisfying. No great sports events are on; I've heard the horrendous news "headlines" five times as my car advances fifty feet; the right-wing talk-show hosts raise in me homicidal tendencies that I thought I had overcome as a teenager; and I can't stand to hear another commercial that offers me no money down and low borrowing rates to buy a brand new Pontiac. "You won't have to make a payment until 2007." The freeway news comes on and I discover that "an overturned big rig" has caused a backup on the 10 for approximately eight miles. "They're trying to clear the lanes."

I switch to the "more stimulating talk-radio" station and instead of Rush Limbaugh or Dr. Laura pontificating on how we should live, I hear an authoritative voice speaking directly to my immediate concern.

"Do you suffer from smog?" the pleasant and sincere trained voice asks.

"You bet your ass," I respond, hoping other drivers aren't looking and seeing me talking to no one.

"Do your eyes burn, water, and drip?"

"Yes, yes," I scream at the dashboard, thinking that some urban planner will reveal a new scheme for limiting auto traffic by reviving rapid public transport.

"If smog attacks your eyes, we have the answer," the reassuring actor's voice continues.

"I can't believe this," I tell myself. "Someone has come up with a cure for smog in Los Angeles and I haven't heard about it?"

"Try Visine," the voice commands. "Visine relieves the symptoms of smog with no harmful effects. You don't have to keep suffering. Go to your nearby pharmacy and ask for Visine."

"What a great way to deal with smog," I tell myself. Individualize a common problem. All I have to tell myself is that smog is my problem and I have a way to overcome it.

Wow! I feel giddy. Maybe it's the amount of carbon monoxide I've inhaled. "No," I tell myself, "I've just gained an insight into coping with the world: first, think of social problems as personal; second, buy something!" If I only had Visine next to me on the empty passenger seat, I could drop the fluid into each smoldering eye and feel immediate relief. Of course, getting off the freeway to find a pharmacy isn't all that easy. I'm in the far left lane, not the empty HOV lane which requires two people in a car (you pay a $271 fine for using it without the required number of passengers).

I begin to snake my way toward the right, provoking other motorists, who also miss their Visine, to honk, hold up middle fingers, or shake fists. I pray that none of them goes for his or her gun. The road rage stories on LA freeways have become legendary. Some drivers, clutching cell phones or talking into dangling microphones connected to their phones, look at me as if some intruding alien had usurped freeway space. Come to think of it, if I had my cell phone, I too could be talking to someone. Perhaps my shrink might even answer the phone and listen to me describe my fears and anxieties. The shrink charges the same fees for phone consults as he does for couch sessions, by the way. He, like most Angelenos, has adapted profitably to the vicissitudes of daily commuting life.

I inch, slide, and bully my way rightward toward the exit lane. In less than ten minutes I have advanced several hundred yards and now wait to enter the heavy but maneuverable street traffic. My edemic eyes and mutinous sinuses impel me to the nearest branch of a chain pharmacy, one of those two-acre stores that stock shelves with almost everything a smog-suffering person could ever want, from shoes and socks to birth-control devices. But try to find someone who works there outside of the minimum-wage checkout-counter teenager!

I locate Visine in the eye care section, right next to dental needs and across from the liquor counter (there's a thought!). Next to it, I see Murine and a dozen other drops designed for red, sore, and itchy eyes. I read the label and discover that Visine is loaded with chemicals that sound as toxic as the fumes my eyes have been absorbing on the freeway.

I go to the tiny pharmacy section of the vast pharmacy and wait patiently for the white-coated professional to answer my question.

"What's the difference," I ask in my most naïve tone of voice, "between Visine and Liquid Tears?"

"Oh," says the pharmacist, "Visine is a chemical mixture and Liquid Tears just lubricates dry and sore eyes. If I were you," he whispers, "I'd stick with the Tears."

Decisions! I bought both. "What a way to deal with smog," I thought to myself . . . Eye drops, nose drops, cough drops. Deal with air pollution as an individual problem. Treat yourself and forget about the gang of criminals in and around the auto and highway industries who planned and executed the destruction of public transportation, the building of massive freeways and the uglification of everything around them. In the film *Who Framed Roger Rabbit?* which played its first run a decade ago, a syndicate led by a cartoon character plotted the destruction of the Los Angeles street railway system and the subsequent building of the freeway system.

The film's punchline, only a toon could have thought of something so ridiculous, turned out to be reality. The CEOs of transportation, construction, and gasoline companies made billions by depriving the public of its collective wealth and literally forcing each individual to drive a car.

After inhaling lots of poisonous gas while stuck in traffic snarls, I think that the individuals who created this social monstrosity now sell their outrageous model of modern urban life as the best of all possible worlds.

The Los Angeles model of congestion and nervous breakdowns or road rage envelops every metropolitan area. Thus far, no criminal charges have been filed against those corporate and political criminals who conspired to make us suffer this aberration of human behavior called "freeways." And don't hold your breath—or maybe you should when the smog level increases.

October 2002

A Global Warming Sermon in Dialogue

When national leaders have no concept of the past, they tend to view
the future as simply an infinite projection of the present.
—Irving Socrates, nineteenth-century tailor

Reading the morning papers, with Israelis and Palestinians, Indians and
Pakistanis killing each other, bad environmental news about air, water,
and global warming, and terrible economic news from Africa and
throughout the third world, I sigh in despair. I wonder what the USA,
the richest and most powerful, could or should be doing about these
issues, some of which threaten the stability of the world and bode ill for
the future, if we have one.

Our chief executive, a friendly and compassionate man according to
those who know him, has not made a reputation for possessing deeply
reflective qualities. He apparently relaxes by playing video golf and
avoids drinking by exercising regularly.

But he does respect the opinion of experts, especially those that have
gone through the vetting process by the conservative Republican
guardians of the status quo. So, when I read in June 2002 that George
W. Bush had finally accepted the findings of his own scientific committee
that global warming is a fact, and a dangerous one at that, I felt elated—
for a few seconds.

The June 21, 2002 *Guardian* reports that climate change is actually
good, if you're a pest or parasite and want to attack wildlife with weakened immune systems. The president told us simply that we should just
"adjust" to global warming. It's a fact of life. Climates will change. It
could mean the end of the earth and that moron in the White House tells
us to adjust to it?

"Hey," I shouted to my wife, "you better buy the strongest underarm
deodorant you can find, unless of course those morally impeccable corporate leaders voluntarily decide to limit greenhouse gas emissions."

"Huh?" she said. "Are you crazy? Corporate CEOs have gene im-
plants making it impossible for them to think about anything beyond
their own fortunes. What are you talking about anyway?"

"I'm trying to follow the president's advice and modify our behavior in order to survive the effects of global warming. If the temperature keeps rising, one thing we'll need to keep our relationship civil is more underarm protection, if you don't mind me using the commercial euphemism. I'm not going to advise women on what else you'll need to do."

"Get serious," my wife demanded, "global warming doesn't just mean that you'll perspire more heavily in the future. Face it, parts of Antarctica have broken up and have melted into the ocean. It means that as polar ice caps melt, sea-water levels rise. Floods, droughts, tidal waves, and yearly El Niños ensue."

She went on about the threat of mosquito-carried viruses that cause Rift Valley fever and hit cattle and humans. "I read that when the world gets hotter the mosquito population multiplies as do the diseases they cause and carry. Diseases that were once isolated to tropical zones would infect temperate climates.[10] A warmer world," she said, "means a sicker world as well."

"Hold on," I responded. "Look at the bright side. We've made progress educating our Republican presidents. In the 1980s, Ronald Reagan called people concerned with preserving forests against clearcutting a bunch of sissies."

"Yeah," she retorted, "real progress! While Americans elect ignorant presidents, the deterioration of the environment continues apace. It's a result of modern production methods. Look at the east coast of China, the US-Mexico border, the burgeoning third-world cities where millions of underpaid workers manufacture electronic junk, including communication instruments, clothes, and jogging accoutrements. Look at the mounting poverty, the falling life expectancy in parts of the world, the absence of medical care and education as we in the rich part of the world—and not all of the people here enjoy those things—drown all of our preoccupations in mindless consumerism."

"That's quite a speech," I remarked. "I bet you voted for Ralph Nader."

"And," she continued, oblivious to my sarcasm, "what world leaders have the courage or wit to stand up and face these monumental and compelling tasks? W prattles on about his precious little war against terrorism, England's Tony Blair can't wait to kiss W's you know what..."

I interrupted her harangue. "I heard that doctors found a foreign object in W's colon last month. It was a piece of Tony Blair's nose."

"Ha," she continued without laughing. "Putin in Russia, the Chinese,

Japanese, French, Italian, German, and Canadian leaders put together don't equal one halfway decent statesman."

"So," I asked, "who would you suggest? Fidel Castro certainly addresses those themes. Would you name him president of the world?"

"What I'm asking for is the impossible yet necessary. We need a brain, some person or persons who can demand a halt to the current dynamics of destruction and begin a new process that allows us to sustain life on this planet. Do you realize," she asked, "that more than half the world's population, more than three billion people, live below the UN established standards for minimum income? And the US government stands as the foremost obstacle to redistributing income from rich to poor people in this country and in the world."[11]

I couldn't stand to listen anymore. I agreed with her. But what to do? Brilliant graduates of Harvard and Yale Business Schools use their intelligence and education to obtain better bottom-line figures for global corporations. Indeed, CEOs of major corporations, not just Enron and WorldCom, have abandoned law, ethics, and everyday notions of common decency for the purpose of increasing their own fortunes. They argue that cooking corporate books gives them great profit. Hey, that's what investors want for their retirement packages: money without working for it. I wandered outside.

My wife followed me. "It's time to do something," she demanded.

"You mean take out the garbage? Change the oil in the car? Mop the kitchen floor?"

"No, silly," she laughed, "I mean it's time for people to stand up and get involved. It's our world and we can't afford to leave it to those waspy Prizzis in the White House and State House in Florida. The Bush family and its entourage, the CEOs of the giant corporations and banks, have created an unsustainable world. We have all fallen into the consumer trap. It's time we became citizens again. Instead of stressing over how we're going to make the next payment on the next appliance, we can get back into politics. Remember how much fun we all had in the 1960s and 1970s, getting civil rights, stopping the Vietnam War, changing peoples' values?"

"Hey," I said. "What got into you? You remember sex, drugs, and rock 'n roll?"

We went back inside and she put on a Bob Marley tape. "Get up. Stand up. Fight for your rights."

August 2002

An Anza Borrego Odyssey

The glacier knocks in the cupboard
The desert sighs in the bed
And the crack in the tea-cup opens
A lane to the land of the dead
WH Auden, "One Evening"

I.
The desert poses questions
We do not walk
Noses to the ground
We do not know
Who or what has
Traversed the ancient sand
Built upon its floor
Deserts have no doubts
Men claim its turf
Mine! Call it law

II
Empty cans and bottles
Open-mouthed and silent
Left behind scream messages
To weary desert cacti
Unprotected against winds by
Kleenex dirtying dusty sage
No matter sand whispers
The desert will prevail

III.
I a natural contaminator
feel captivated miniscule obscured
by bulbous burly boulders
I protected by calluses

Dismiss the rocks suffering
affronts of manufactured metal
rusty cans vying for
attention with streaks of
bloody iron copper gold
oblivious to flying gum
wrappers flitting toward flash
flooding waters denying eternal
lodging for millennial rocks
The desert poses questions

IV.
One hundred years ago
they decided to preserve
His Domain for heirs
who could claim it
How to stop Nature
Whisking away trees roots
insects animals used condoms
raging waters hurl rocks
twist winds torture pollen
Deracinate clutching grasping vines
Deserts love hot suns

V.
Winter signals scorpions rattlers
tarantulas poisonous gila monsters
Seek shelter under quilted
geological faults ominous holes
Layers of inception's abyss
I tread on them
Fearing that my boots
Will awaken anger entice
Fanged creatures to emerge
Strike fearless campers ignorant
Of Nature's creatures pouring
poison into slumber's ear
the desert doesn't sleep

January 2002

Mount Whitney Towers over Death Valley, but Death Valley Doesn't Look Up to Whitney

Wow, a vacation! The teenager has gone off to stay with a sib. "Until the rise of American advertising," paraphrasing Gore Vidal, "it never occurred to anyone anywhere in the world that the teenager was a captive in a hostile world of adults."[12] Maybe we owe the very existence of modern adolescence to the desperate need to create markets. Adolescence, created as an advertising gimmick? Maybe the advertisers created pimples as well! Watch Reality TV and throw up!

I anxiously surf the dial hoping for something that will place me in my world, help me integrate my thoughts and feelings, and not alienate me further. The shows on the commercial channels appear to validate Vidal's observation that TV has become "so desperately hungry for material that they're scraping the top of the barrel."[13]

The answer to tension at work, freeway jams, John Ashcroft's threat to further invade my privacy, and George W. Bush's launching an unprovoked war, lies in taking a vacation away from it all. Imagine, we will take three days to just hang out and stare at Nature's wonders with all the awe they deserve!

A trip to Death Valley, we decide, will afford us views of natural phenomena and a chance to breathe clean air. As for pollution in LA, as Robert Orben noted, if not "for our lungs there'd be no place else to put it."[14]

On some days I think that even the rocks in my garden will succumb to the contamination.

Drive north on a Friday afternoon, as the radio alert on the "all-news station" reminds us, "You'll find the 15 north clogged with Christmas vacationers en route to Las Vegas and people hot to get to the mall to take advantage of those after-Christmas sales." Angelenos love Vegas, the creation of Bugsy Siegel, an insane Jewish gangster who predicted that millions of people would visit gambling casinos and entertainment palaces in the desert.

"Hey, I get a suite of rooms, free food and drinks, see great shows, and sit beside the pool," an acquaintance tells me. "All I have to do is gamble at the high stakes tables."

"And?" I ask.

"I won once," he said. "So it costs me a few grand every month or two. I can't resist the idea of getting a free hotel room."

Another friend says he goes for the shows. "Maybe I drop a few hundred into the slots and on the roulette table. But seeing Wayne Newton at Caesar's Palace! That's worth it."

We turn north onto California 395 and enter the Mojave Desert, or what should be renamed the "Mojave Desert Housing Development for People Who Can't Afford Homes in Reasonable Places." Billboards advertise three- and four-bedroom "units" for sale for the low "100s." "Buy the house of your dreams," one billboard entices. I remember Bob Kaufman demanding that "the government stop cluttering up our billboards with highways."

"You want to take a look?" I say suggestively to my wife.

"Forget it," she says. "Why would you want to live in the actual and cultural desert where temperatures rise over one hundred degrees for several months a year, where you're hours from a place where they show decent movies, where there's no theater, no culture? And besides, we have enough trouble maintaining one 'unit.'"

We pass "Okie Ray's Museum." But it's closed. We laugh. Is this the heritage of the Okies, the farmers who had to leave the Oklahoma dust bowl and came to California, what Woody Guthrie sang about as the "garden of Eden as long as you got the do-re-mi." I wonder if the museum contains photos of the real Okies or just posters of Henry Fonda as Tom Joad in the film version of John Steinbeck's *The Grapes of Wrath*.

Towns are few and far between in the Mojave as they should be. But developers have somehow gotten access to enough water to build "communities" in this unfriendly terrain and they advertise "dream houses."

"More like a nightmare," I say to my wife. An occasional ranch dots the base of the mountain range, a maintenance shed, a railroad repair installation. The arid landscape extends over the high desert, the tough cactus, the Joshua trees, the infrequent jackrabbit; coyote, lizard, and the hungry crow find lean pickings in winter.

But the ancient craggy structures in Death Valley, the lowest spot in the country, endure. And we, as tourists on earth, visit Badwater, 282 feet below the level of the ocean's surface. We walk on the crusted salt floor amidst other tourists from Europe and Asia and a few of our own.

I think about the phenomenon of driving several hours to experience the world as it was—well, as it has evolved. Evolution must include the Coors and Bud Light bottles lying as dramatic pieces of strewn sculpture in the vast craterlike landscape. A vicious-looking cactus, less than three feet high, has caught a white plastic shopping bag on one of its powerful thorns. The bag flutters frantically in the wind, as if trying to escape the ancient spines that have pierced its thin polyethylene surface. Will the flapping cease before the cactus dies? How many decades or centuries will this contest endure? Should we add the history of plastic bags to the overall history of Death Valley, not to mention aluminum cans? Until 1849, history in Death Valley, according to the various pamphlets written and distributed by the National Park Service, consisted of the history of rocks, mountains, flash floods, flora, and fauna.

Human history (that is, white history) began on Christmas Day 1849 when gold-seekers (forty-niners) entered the space occupied by Panamint Indians. What happened during the centuries of life that these indigenous people occupied and lived in the area presumably doesn't qualify as real history.

Appropriately, caravans of lucre-hungry white men thought they had found a shortcut to the California gold area. The successive caravans of miners found some silver deposits and other precious metals and with each strike new settlements arose in the valley. But Nature, in the form of extreme heat and dryness in summer, drove the tough pioneers away.

Many miners died seeking silver and even gold, a futile search. The rocks implore the greedy prospector, with signs that metals galore exist inside them. The yellow flickers, the greens and rusts, signal gold, copper, and iron ore. And, of course, the rocks did have traces of all these wonderful metals, but the economics of extracting them did not coincide with the supply.

The only enduring mining, extracting boron, from which is derived borax ("white gold of the desert"), did make some people rich. But wealth alone did not suffice to tie human settlements to the harsh climate. By the 1880s the Harmony Borax Works began to send 20-mule-team borax trains with loads of almost 50,000 pounds on their trek across the desert to the railroad in Mojave some 160 miles away. In 1890, the factory moved to the Calico Mountains, closer to the railroad.

Old history told to tourists who visit these relics on bus tours from Vegas or in rented cars. Members of the desert club go hunting, mountain climbers test their stamina and heart, nature lovers kvell over the moonscape, and, like us, eventually head back home, having seen a piece of relatively untouched Nature. That is, nature in its extreme form is too hot to touch.

Like Whitney towering above it, Death Valley signals untouchable power. Unfortunately, most people come away from it thinking about what a nice day or weekend they spent "out there" before returning home to "civilization."

One day, however, our scientists may figure out how to conquer these remote and forbidding areas so that we can turn them into more lucrative tourist sites or, better still, factories and office buildings. The materials to make these modern production and residential facilities all originate in Nature. They just look kind of different. I guess that's progress!

December 2002

In the Death Valley museums, tourists see how the Indians who lived in the area dried their meat into jerky. That was before chemicals.

Diseased Meat?—Could Be Wurst!

For those out there who still eat meat
I don't want to blow the horn
Nor change the eaters' basic taste
From porterhouse to corn
You've read about the scandals
That doctors now avow
Worse than hoof and mouth disease
It's the epidemic of mad cow
It seems that the meat producers
To make profits soar and leap
Fed dead parts to live animals
I refer to brains of poor dead sheep
They ship them round the world
As large growers are wont to do
They pack them tight in cattle cars
From Great Britain to Beirut
The butcher shops must buy this meat
They really have no choice
The companies stay focused
And consumers have no voice
They cram the cows together
few inspectors check their health
The companies stay focused
to magnify their wealth
They lobby against regulations
deny blame for all misdeeds
Its profits not meat that matters
that's the industry's vital creed
Back in our great country
millions wretched from *e. coli* food
eating assembly line burgers
that we equate with common good
The famous golden arches loom

Over fast food shacks galore
Burger king and junior Carl's
Proliferate like live spores
But now the scare that Europe knows
Has finally reached our land
We suffer from our own disease
Our madness is quite grand
I conclude this tale of animal woe
by alerting all my friends
Lay off Big Macs and KFCs
Remember that means have ends
Big companies care about making dough
Not giving you healthy regimes
Be wary of meat you don't raise yourself
The result could be wurst than it seems

March 2001

Exporting the Best Chemicals
the Stomach Can Absorb

I fell asleep reading an article in some coverless magazine that I grabbed in the hotel lobby. The author crowed about how successful we Americans have become in exporting our ways of life, our basic cultural values. I missed my dinner.

In the early morning, with raging hunger pains stabbing at my gut, I broke a vow. First, I ascertained that no one I knew had seen me. Then, I snuck into the line at McDonald's at the San Jose Airport, the only place open before 6 AM. With my head down, hunger pains screaming, I did what I had sworn never to do, I muttered "Egg McMuffin" to the Spanish-speaking server who screamed back to the serving area, "Un huevo mamoofan."

"Joo wan cofi?" she asked.

I declined and in less than 10 seconds she grabbed a hot package placed in its proper slot by an unseen hand behind the counter, slid it into a bag, handed it to me, and motioned me toward the cash register, mumbling in heavily accented English, "Hah a gray one."

Another Spanish-speaking person extracted less than $3 for this steamy bag and pointed to the condiments section when I asked for ketchup. "Senk you," she said. She tried to smile, but the effort only accentuated the pain in her face.

I wondered how long she had been in the United States. According to Eric Schlosser, about one out of every eight workers has at some point been employed by McDonald's. In his *Fast Food Nation*, Schlosser estimated that some 3.5 million people work in the fast-food service industry, making them the largest group of minimum-wage earners.

Without looking carefully at the contents, I unwrap and smother the ingredients in ketchup and then pick a remote table in the dining area. I left the minimum-wage area to sit amongst the higher-paid servicers of the corporate world.

Around me men and women peer into their *Wall Street Journals*, which they have arranged aside the McDonald's wrappers. Not one person looks at the food he or she is eating.

Then I stare at the contents of my fare: a grey slice of something, supposedly sausage, stares back. A gluey orange substance—cheese?—has sort of melted over part of it, covering what is probably an egg that looks as if it surrendered. The grease from the grey thing has soaked into the muffin. My hunger pains and my reason have begun a toe-to-toe battle. "Eat this untidy heap and you'll never be the same," screams Jean-Jacques Rousseau from deep inside my head.

"G'wan, try it," shouts the hunger pain. "It won't kill you. You haven't eaten since yesterday's lunch."

I tell Rousseau to go to sleep and slide the steamy apparatus into my mouth. I try to discern the nature of the elements on which my teeth masticate. The fake cheese or whatever sticks to the roof of my mouth like peanut butter, but it has a nonfood taste. "What could it be?" I ask myself.

"It tastes as if it's already been eaten," I conclude. "Maybe this isn't food," I think. "Maybe I'm eating technology." That's it! I've failed to use my critical sensibilities. I think of the redneck joke: Fast food is hitting a deer at 65 mph. I've just filled my mouth with taste-provoking esters, manufactured in bulk in labs along the New Jersey Turnpike. Chemists and other technicians inject this ersatz concoction into food that now oozes past my tongue and slides effortlessly down the hatch. I have just swallowed modern technology, a commonplace for hundreds of millions twenty-four hours a day throughout the world. I have become one with people of all ages, races, ethnic persuasions, and occupations. I have quit the slow- and joined the fast-food eaters of the world. Will the slow-food eaters die off like dinosaurs?

The fast-food meal, an oxymoron, promoted as a complete breakfast, redefines eating. In Mexico, Europe, large parts of Asia, and even Africa, fast-food operations have proliferated. Advertised as an exciting novelty, with new treats for taste buds, the ubiquitous burger, chicken, fries, and taco meals have established themselves as part of the cultural landscape.

The Omaha family flies American Airlines to Paris, rents a Hertz car, which Daddy drives to the Paris Holiday Inn, and then goes out for its first authentic French meal at the McDonald's nearby. Mom does buy some gear to show her friends when they return, material proof that they actually went to Paris.

Indeed, fast food has become universal and has thus accomplished its marketing (corporate) purpose by aiding and abetting the cause of increased productivity without forcing a wage hike. It allows the workforce to place calories and certain other ingredients into its collective body in the most rapid time possible at a minimum expense. The construction worker that had previously allotted thirty minutes or more for lunch can now stash a Big Mac and fries, washed down with a Coke or so-called shake in fifteen minutes or less. He never has to leave his car.

The breakthroughs in the technology of fast food allow the franchiser to order the standardized ingredients from a central production facility, use standardized cooking and cleaning instruments, and, of course, employ minimum-wage teenage or foreign labor to keep costs down. The fast-food servers make no tips, thus keeping the price down for workers who otherwise would have to add fifteen to twenty percent to their meal expenses.

Fast food also contributes directly to economic growth. According to Schlosser, Americans now spend more money on fast food ($110 billion last year) than they do on higher education. They spend more on fast food than on movies, books, magazines, newspapers, videos, and recorded music—combined. And most people can buy most meals for $5 or less.

Fast-food restaurants, like microwave ovens, allow women, who once cooked every night for their families, to herd hubby and kids into one of the myriad plastic places that smell of cooking oil being heated to high temperatures and mixed with other material. These impersonal sites serve a variety of products kept warm under lamps that the menu promotes as breakfast, lunch, or dinner. The brightly colored signs inside claim that you can even purchase extra-value meals.

Schlosser argues that in addition the fast-food industry spreads the worst of capitalism. Among the bad values it promotes, he lists "hostility to workers' rights, along with a dehumanizing emphasis on mass production and uniformity at the expense of meaningful worker training and autonomy."

Back at the airport, an airline employee announces pre-boarding, a strange airport code that means disabled people or those with small children should get on the plane. At 6 AM my flight has no kids or disabled people, a fact that the airline employees had observed when the passengers checked in.

I stuff the remains of my McMuffin into the bag and push it into one of the pervasive wastebaskets. Salesmen and techies natter into their cell phones asking about prices, quoting figures, and exchanging tips with someone at the home office on the East Coast. The unremitting metal object held to their ear has become a cruel life-prop.

How did we ever live without them? Like fast food and other wonderful gadgets and toys, the cell phone allows them to be more productive, or for someone to extract more labor from them. Hey, people can eat fast food and cut deals on cell phones at the same time they board a plane to cut another deal and have another fast-food meal on landing!

On the plane, the pre-takeoff ritual begins with announcements from the head flight attendant. "I'll call you from LA," my seatmate shouts into his cell phone. He then attaches it to his belt and shuts down his laptop. I feel like an oddball, without phone or laptop, albeit I have shared an ingestion experience with most of the other passengers. The captain reassures us that everything is normal, the temperature is sixty-one degrees, the flight will take one hour and five minutes, flying conditions are good, so sit back and relax.

Easy for him to say. He probably didn't eat an Egg McMuffin. I wonder if what I just ate contained genetically modified material. How many Egg McMuffins would it require to develop stomach or colon cancer, with or without genetic modification? Is this Jewish neurosis or practical science?

The McDonald's story didn't end when the plane landed. My teenage daughter waited for me in her car. On the car floor lay several McDonald's wrappers; some, by olfactory estimation, had been there for some time. I disciplined myself and said nothing.

McDonald's has become standard teenage fare. It has shaped my daughter's taste buds, at least until she is open to having them reshaped. How pernicious this technology becomes as it fashions food aesthetics while it prolongs work hours. Hey, I can well understand why corporate executives eagerly export this kind of culture.

June 2003

Fast food is to haute cuisine what Las Vegas is to urban culture.

Las Vegas: Bush's America

My wife and I celebrated my birthday in Las Vegas—as a patriotic act, of course. Where else could one spend money as quickly and see such over-sized American flags, which made me identify even more with my country. If I couldn't understand the symbolism in substantial red, white, and blue banners flying over casinos and car lots, a bumper sticker reassured me: "Las Vegas is America." Notice how no one ever says "US flag," or sings "God Bless the US!"

My father used to call it Lost Wages. For five decades it has lured the tourists, the desperate, the bored, and dissatisfied. To the high-rollers, Vegas offers anything: good food at low prices, professional sex workers who will satisfy one's kinky but clearly secondary urges, secondary, that is, to spending your big-time money at the blackjack and crap tables.

On the street, young Mexican men hand out magazines and flyers adorned with naked women. "Female entertainers, topless clubs, totally nude bars, personals, swingers, and more! Girls Girls Girls!" A "$90 special" printed on a $90 bill gives a phone number and a Web site, and promises the hottest girls in Las Vegas.

"Try to imagine your daughter's face on those handbills," my wife indignantly tells me. I look at the Mexican men handing them out and wonder how much they get for handing out the porn.

Las Vegas stands for naked unabashed lust for money, which literally screams at the visitor to the strip, or the airport, or the lunch counters, where the ubiquitous slots (once known as one-armed bandits) promise you large sums of money, never mind virgins in heaven. Imagine a new Disneyland theme park after it has received a massive dose of steroids! Or, a large drainage tube inserted into the veins of the poor, but instead of suctioning toxic secretions, it drains all of the disposable income. That's Vegas.

See Vegas and you don't have to travel around the world. You can stay at the New York, New York and eat at the Carnegie deli. Visit the Paris or Venetian hotels and walk the rues and vias, all recreated in stucco, and, as Groucho Marx said, "Boy, can you get stucko." Shop at the expensive boutiques, eat crepes, and sample the haute cuisine or fresh pasta—experience Europe without going there.

To get to any of the attractions, we had to pass through a casino, of course. But if you maintain iron discipline and don't take too much money with you (and can resist the temptation to visit the tempting ATM machines) you will see that Vegas has recreated the wonders of the world. You can visit the Eiffel Tower, the Pyramids, and the Taj Mahal without leaving our own wonderful country.

One night we dined at Red Square at the Mandalay Bay, where a desecrated statue of Lenin stands at the door. Apparently, customers objected to seeing the face of Russian communism's father and the restaurant owners "modified" the massive sculpture to oblige the ideologically minded customers who couldn't appreciate high camp as art. Anyway, the blini were delicious.

But one can easily lose one's appetite at the casinos, where mostly poorly dressed women feed coins of all denominations into the ever-hungry mouths of the slots, waiting for the big payoff. Their eyes appear glazed. I wondered if any of them got carpal tunnel syndrome from the repetitive motions, punctuated only by the occasional sip of their cocktail from the scantily clad waitresses who push the free booze to the already tipsy gamblers.

The blinking neon signs announce how many million you can win if you hit the jackpot and the hypnotic electronic resonance of the machines syncopates their beeps to the steady thud of New Age disco rhythms. The unvarying cacophony challenges all rational sensibilities. I ask a weary woman in a cheap dress, carrying a plastic bucket full of quarters, how long it had taken her to win the jackpot. "Oh," she replied, "I've been here since, gosh, it must be three days."

"Did you win a lot," I asked.

"No, I lost a few thousand," she said. "But at least I got one small jackpot." She must have seen the skepticism in my face when she said. "You know the house has the odds, but you never know when you might get lucky."

Las Vegas continues to grow, and as it grows, it finds itself short on medical and school services for the residents. We drove through the ever-expanding neighborhoods of walled and gated communities where the croupiers and dealers live, along with the plumbers, electricians, masons, and the hundreds of thousands who service this burgeoning metropolis, this gambling capital created by an insane gangster who essentially said,

"Build it, even in the middle of the desert where temperatures reach one hundred twenty degrees, and they will come."

Bugsy Siegel's fantasy now contains nearly a million inhabitants and a very busy McCarren Airport, named after the Senator who authored the infamous McCarren Anti-Immigration act of the 1950s. People come from all over the world to find the American answer to the problem of life, to find the promise of easy money, with God's help. "I'm lucky, I could save up enough to get here," an eighty-seven-year-old man tells me at the five-dollar minimum blackjack table. "I came here from Iowa to see if I could get really lucky."

It's George W. Bush's America, God Bless It.

January 2002

Havana is not the exact antithesis of Las Vegas, but it's as close as one can get in the Western Hemisphere.

Cuba Is Not Las Vegas:
Scenes from a Late Summer Havana Wedding

On the wedding morning, I accompanied the groom from one dollar store to another on an unsuccessful quest for ice. I thought Gabriel Garcia Marquez might have been wrong in his first line in *One Hundred Years of Solitude*: "Many years later, as he faced the firing squad, Colonel Aureliano Buendia was to remember that distant afternoon when his father took him to discover ice."[15] In post-Soviet Cuba, ice has been invented, but eludes the open market.

We called several friends, who offered us their meager freezer stash, but hardly enough cumulatively to stretch for one hundred people. Finally, a friend of a friend of the groom knew a *babalao* (Santeria priest) who knew a man who worked in an ice factory who in turn agreed to sell us the needed amount for about five times the going price. We made the transaction. Hey, how often does a guy get married!

"Cubans understand privatization," the groom explained as we continued our shopping preparations for the wedding party. "Someone steals the people's ice, privatization, and sells it back to the people at a very high price. Unfortunately, we have to rely on it when the state can't meet the needs of the people."

Since the collapse of the Soviet Union more than a decade ago, the Cuban government has had to cut back on its cradle-to-grave social security guarantees. Third-world states are understandably broke—look at Argentina after getting IMF'd—and the once all-encompassing ration book now supplies only a small percentage of what Cubans need for daily sustenance and minimum comfort.

"So," explained a political science professor at the pre-wedding party, "we have the phenomenon of illegal privatization, a variation on the concept in capitalist countries. In Mexico, for example, the government sells public property cheaply to a private company, usually connected with key ruling clique members, and then watches in silence as the corporate executives of the company loot its treasury, cut back on service, and let the property run down. When the company no longer finds profit in the property, the state either buys it back with a large profit going to the company or subsidizes the property it had sold supposedly for the purpose of creating efficiency and making the country more attractive for foreign investment. Or take your president, who wants to turn social security into an enterprise where his rich friends can make fifteen percent off poor peoples' pensions for investing it. It's simply private theft of public property and that's what capital is interested in."

Unlike Mexico, Cuba has proved less than attractive to major multinational capital despite its highly educated and skilled workforce. Investment has gone into tourism, mining, and some agriculture, but no *maquiladoras*, factories where foreign capital wants to control the workforce and dispose of the industrial waste on the cheap.

Instead, Havana, a city of some two million residents dramatizes the ironies of life under socialism in the age of corporate globalization. "We produce little and consume much, although not as much as we would like to consume. We're a city of parasites," a friend informs me. "But it's not our fault. It's the way the system has evolved. We're stuck in a time warp. I'm not referring to the old American cars on the street or the ancient American refrigerators that somehow still function in the houses. I don't know what we're waiting for. No one will save us. The Spanish screwed us for centuries and the Americans for sixty years. We always complained about the Soviet Union although in all honesty they gave us so much and I can't think of what we gave them. Maybe we provided them with a good reputation for socialism, which they were sorely lacking. Fidel was a master pickpocket. Really, for thirty years we took their oil, weapons, food, education, technicians, and gave them some sugar and cigars. I guess we like to complain. We're babies, taken care of by our mothers, then by our mother, the state, and, of course, the greatest mother of them all, Fidel."

The Cuban government allows one wedding cake per marriage at the state bakery but for booze we stop at the dollar store in front of the five-star Spanish-owned Sol Melia Cohiba Hotel, a joint venture with the Cuban government. A checker compares our receipt to the items in our plastic shopping bags on the way out. I don't see the usual hustlers outside trying to buy cash register receipts. In March 2002, at the same store a man offered me a dollar for a receipt for some ham, cheese, beer, and cooking oil. Presumably, he worked for one of the *paladares*, private restaurants, and used the receipt to show the tax collector that he had spent the money for supplies, thereby owing the state less taxes. Ah, the pitfalls of moving ever so slowly toward cockroach capitalism!

A hot, lazy August Saturday brings people out to the Malecon, the avenue protected by a seawall from the Caribbean. Kids and adults fish, neck, catch the breeze, and occasionally hustle a sightseeing tourist or one jogging in the heavy humidity. Some sit on the seawall and gaze northward, as if Florida, just ninety miles away might somehow materialize if one dreamed about it long enough. Some youngsters, in their early twenties, tell me about what a paradise Miami is, how their buddies who made it over on rafts or through smugglers' speedboats wrote them about how wonderful life is under capitalism.

I say nothing about how hard people work in the United States or, unlike Cuba, how easy it is to get fired or laid off. Out of four youths, only one of the young Cubans has a job. None look the slightest bit undernourished or poorly clothed. Two have cars. How they acquire the goods, I don't ask. They, like many Habaneros, have a hustle going. Maybe they rent out a room or apartment without a license, or sell cigars to eager tourists who purchase a $300-plus box of stolen Cohiba Esplendidos for $50? Or, perhaps they're not the genuine article even though they come in the right box and have the stamp and label?

Like the iceman, some cigar workers or supervisors pilfer the peoples' product and sell it for their personal profit. Some people grow animals or plants for sale, build stills, bake cookies and cakes, or rent parts to car owners so they can pass auto inspections. Unofficial small-scale privatization has become a defining institution in contemporary Cuba. Theft of public property is sold back to the public at high prices, just as in the capitalist world where such a phenomenon is legal. In Cuba, when the government gets wise to a privatization scheme it legalizes it, then it taxes it, like room or apartment rentals; or it allows entrepreneurs to convert houses into mini-night clubs, rather than putting the enterprise out of business.

"No es facil," people say, but without the "Ministry of the Street" as some call the schemes to make extra money, life would be truly difficult.

How else can Habaneros maintain a consumption style that contradicts their lack of productivity? "Everyone does it, everyone knows everyone does it, and no one talks about it," said a sociologist friend. "We became accustomed to certain lifestyles, which included not working too hard, and after the Soviet Union collapsed we adjusted through individual hustles, not through a planned or coordinated process. The state maintained its political control by keeping control of the main forces of the economy and did not allow an independent civil society to develop. Fidel never wanted a consumer society to develop here. I agree with him that the third world can't afford it."

But on wedding days, people spend money. Families dressed in their finest waited outside the Wedding Palace. Brides in white gowns and veils and grooms in natty summer suits arrived in ostentatious displays of automobile horn tooting. The couples climbed the two flights, erasing as they ascended the thousands of fingerprints of couples and families who also clutched the old marble banisters. Members of the entourage gazed upward at the spiraling staircase of what had been an old Spanish-style mansion.

The young couple, bride on the arm of her father, groom clutched by his mother choking back tears, then trod the ratty red carpet that had peaked some twenty years ago while a middle-aged man with a three-day growth who could barely suppress a yawn placed a tape of Mozart's "Wedding March" into a boombox. A civil servant read the obligations of the marriage contract as the groom's mother dropped ounces of tears on the already much-rained-on carpet: sharing love, respect, and household and child-care duties. They signed. I wondered how many of the young men even listened to the terms of the contract. I also wondered how many of the young women expected the young men to fulfill their part.

Our wedding party completed a busy Saturday. As the newlyweds entered the shiny rented car a middle-aged drunk ran his tattered auto into their bumper. One of the bride's uncles reached into the car and pulled the keys. The offender could not escape. The bride's brother threatened to punch the man who could barely respond. The brother's girlfriend pried him away, screaming that this was no time for violence. Two surly cops came and the driver navigated his way toward the cop car in a drunken weave. The parents handed the car keys to the cops, saying they didn't want to press charges, but did want to make sure that the drunk would not drive his car in that condition. I wondered if a sticky scene like that would have been so easily solved in the USA.

An hour later, as the sun began to set, the wedding party began. The DJ put the tapes in the boombox; the men and women hired to wait on the tables brought food and drinks. Dancing couples filled the floor of the rented hall on the shore of the Caribbean in the Miramar neighborhood. I went outside to prevent my eardrums from collapsing. Other older (over-fifty) people joined me. We congratulated each other on the wedding, on how the groom would get his degree in computer science, and the bride, already a degree holder, would develop her own hacking abilities. We talked as if Cuba had a clear future. "Who knows what will happen here," one writer said. "We have never known and we never will. We are now more like the rest of the third world, with better health and education, of course, and with a clear understanding of our rights."

"What if the embargo is lifted," I asked.

"Yes," he sighed. "What if? McDonald's in Havana? Obviously, many things will change, but how? We don't know. But in what other country in this world can people look ahead with security? Cuba's insecurity goes with the insecure times everywhere."

The next day, after a very nonstressful passage through Cuban security just as thorough as any US airport, I boarded the American Eagle charter to Miami. On the plane flying over Cuba, I looked down at the fertile island. Cuba is like an airplane in a holding pattern, I think, slowly running out of fuel, with no clear place to land. If it does crash, Cubans will truly join the third world, in all of its misery.

September 2002

5

The Iraq Conundrum

By mid-March 2003, Cubans felt a new anxiety, as President Bush prepared to invade Iraq and who knew how many other countries.

Bush and King Henry—
Similar Birds of Different Feathers

President Bush has a well-deserved reputation among the highbrows as uncultured. While he may not have the intellect to distinguish between Shakespeare and Ogden Nash, he has certainly immersed himself in the culture of power, in the narrowest sense.

For Bush—after 9/11—power means simply command, not responsibility for the consequences of his actions. Indeed, by waging unprovoked war against Iraq, he discarded decades of legal culture established by conservatives. He acted radically, ignoring the wisdom of conservative icon Edmund Burke, "Our patience will achieve more than our force."

Nor did the unrefined wielder of power pause to interpret the soldier Will's words from Henry V before the King does battle at Agincourt. "I am afear'd there are few die well that die in a battle; for how can they charitably dispose of any thing when blood is their argument?" Henry and Bush, both fun-loving princes, who hung out with low-lifes in their youth, fell into their positions as heads of state.

But unlike Bush, Shakespeare's Henry fought alongside his men and respected his enemy. In contrast, after the successful invasion of Iraq, when the resistance to US occupation began, Bush taunted those his army had vanquished. "Bring 'em on," was his response to the growing US body count at a July 2 White House press conference, as if he were John Wayne starring as a US Marshal in Baghdad, Wyoming.

King Henry, however, dealt with consequences. For example, he could have simply claimed the French princess after victory but, instead, thinking of future relations with France, wooed her. Bush, the leader of the world's most prolific military power, after winning against an effectively disarmed third-world nation, did not reestablish the rule of law.

Quite the contrary, he had already amply demonstrated his lack of respect for legality. In his first two years in office he withdrew from more international treaties than any president in US history. After the 9/11 events, he squandered vast international good will by taking a military rather than a judicial path toward "fighting" terrorism. His aggressive western movie stance, his dissing of the United Nations and those allies who disagreed, and his threatening approach to smaller nations who refused one hundred percent obedience gained him and his government worldwide animosity. He has weakened the United Nations.

As US forces illegally invaded and then occupied Iraq, he continued to shred the fabric of world law by ordering the assassination of Uday and Qusai Hussein, the deposed ruler's sons. How much more instructive for the world to have prosecutors present the evidence against these men in international court!

Previous presidential graduates of Harvard and Yale did not elevate assassination to the open and highest level of policy. They kept it covert, fearing its effect on the foundations of law. Albeit sneaky and treacherous, Bush's predecessors understood the repercussions that would result from making coups and murders normal instruments of state policy. Under Bush's culture of power, members of the US Army should feel no shame when their commanders order hundreds of them armed with heavy firepower to execute two men. One wonders if the Israeli assassination method has become contagious!

The media, which adapts in a Darwinian fashion to cultural shifts in the White House, seemed unmoved by this sea change in US policy whereby hunting down an enemy without recourse to trial becomes acceptable behavior. Indeed, the mainstream editorials seemed to accept as legitimate international practice the Hollywood formula of chasing the black hats and killing them.

The Dow Jones Average responded to the murder of Saddam's sons by rising over one hundred points. The president seems unconcerned that his actions might set a precedent. One of his enemies around the world might well copy him and offer a bounty for the heads of his twin daughters. Indeed, Texans especially should understand that. Anyone who has read the "eye for an eye" passage of the Bible will get the point.

But that's not how Bush thinks. Thinks? I have used too strong a word. The nature of Bush's knowledge, his presuppositions, and underlying foundations, can be reduced to one simple word: power. He doesn't understand complicated or even less than complicated ideas, but he does grasp power viscerally. He possesses it. Therefore, he commands. "Leaders lead," he reminded Al Gore during the 2000 presidential debates.

Conservative columnist William Safire has yet to write his Sunday *New York Times Magazine* language column about Bush's epistemology.

I could imagine Safire toasting the president's virtues, loyalty to friends and donors (the same people), and certitude about the conduct of his war of terror.

Critics and partisans alike should avoid certain words to describe Bush's decision-making process. For example, words such as think, study, reflect, calculate, reason, and deduce have little impact on the chief executive. If the president doesn't engage in what we would ordinarily call "thinking"—as in undergoing the mental processes of formulating, reflecting, or pondering—we ought not criticize or praise him for such mental dynamics. For example, who in his right mind would tell Bush to "think the matter through" before making a decision? The exceptions that come to mind would involve him "thinking up a plan to get rich quick" or "thinking himself into a panic" after the 9/11 events. But rather than exercising the power of reason, he feels more comfortable exercising raw power. We have no evidence that Bush conceives actual ideas or draws inferences or calculates consequences.

But so what? He's not an intellectual and doesn't pretend to affairs of the mind. An unnamed White House official told inquiring journalists regarding Bush's apparent lapse on the yellow cake uranium clause in the State of the Union speech, "The president is not a fact checker."

When he said in Cincinnati, Ohio, on October 7, 2002 that "The evidence indicates that Iraq is reconstituting its nuclear weapons program," did he ask for facts? When he claimed in his January 28, 2003 State of the Union Address, that "Our intelligence officials estimate that Saddam Hussein had the materials to produce as much as 500 tons of sarin, mustard, and VX nerve agent," and "The British government has learned that Saddam Hussein recently sought significant quantities of uranium from Africa," did he ask any questions of his intelligence specialists?

The unnamed White House official might have added that the president doesn't check facts because he doesn't care about them. George W. Bush seems to have a characterological disinterest in what scientists consider the core of knowledge. Indeed, Bush seems to view facts as distractions in the face of what he knows to be good and right. Such a mindset might well have led him to invade Iraq.

I don't think the president ignored facts presented by the CIA that cast a dubious light on his *weltanschauung*. The facts just whizzed on by. He knows, in his gut, right from wrong, good from bad. Why listen when you know the answer?

He has surrounded himself with neocon policy analysts, people who conservative pundit James Pinkerton said, possessed more books than common sense, let alone actual military experience. Disregarding prudence, precedent and honesty, they went off—or, more precisely, sent others off—tilting at windmills in Iraq, chasing after illusions of Saddam Hussein's weapons of mass destruction and false hope about Iraqi enthusiasm for Americanism, and hoping that reality would somehow catch up with their theory. The problem, of course, is that wars are more about bloodletting than book learning (*Newsday* July 19, 2003).

Bush apparently did not understand that his advisers had exaggerated or perhaps invented facts that would bolster their arguments for making war against Iraq. They persuaded the president by appealing to his gut feelings. Since neither he nor his key Cabinet advisers thought to check facts, they all went along with the fabrication.

So, I conclude, Bush didn't lie because he didn't know the truth to begin with. Indeed, he had no interest in what intellectuals or scholars, lawyers or scientists might call discernible evidence. He simply ordered the generals to attack, after his Secretary of Defense Donald Rumsfeld micromanaged and second-guessed the Pentagon's plan of action.

Likewise, does Bush realize that he has spent the US surplus, bankrupted the Treasury, and created the largest annual deficit in US history? Under his watch more than two million Americans have so far lost their jobs.

While Bush praises our troops, his budget reduces benefits for war veterans. The man who campaigned as a fiscal conservative has led the nation to the biggest annual spending increases in US history. The man who attributed 9/11 to "them" hating "us" because we're free has removed more freedoms for Americans than any other president, via his Attorney General John Ashcroft's use of the Patriot Act and his Homeland Security Secretary Tom Ridge's understanding of security as incompatible with freedom.

Is he aware of any of these "accomplishments?" Does he know that his "assertion that the war began because Iraq did not admit inspectors appeared to contradict the events leading up to war this spring," as the July 15, 2003 *Washington Post* put it. "Hussein had, in fact, admitted the inspectors," the *Post* reminds us "and Bush had opposed extending their work because he did not believe them effective."

Like the Shakespearean King, Bush assigns blame for the war on others. Henry sends French King Charles a message: "Deliver up the crown, and . . . take mercy/On the poor souls for whom this hungry war/

Opens his vasty jaws; and on your head/Turns he the widows' tears, the orphans' cries" (2.4.103–106). As if Charles somehow forced him into aggression!

Similarly, Bush blamed Saddam. Don't bother him with facts since they do not appear to determine his judgments. I shall refrain from calling him a liar and table my idea for a bumper sticker that says "At least he didn't lie about sex."

July 2003

Don't Get Distracted by Cameron Diaz's Acne or Talk of War

"What's this Bush Administration really about?" a frustrated student asked me.

Good question! I suggested that he look into the clever manipulators, led by White House chief strategist Karl Rove, who have woven together a novel coalition of voracious looters and naked imperialists. By employing styles and methods of bullying, secrecy, and downright prevarication, they have developed a unique political mating process in which the national security mavens bond with religious Christian and Jewish zealots, and fanatic gun lovers cuddle with anti-abortion and death penalty advocates while the rest of us get truly fucked.

Former Defense Policy Board Chairman Richard Perle[1] and Deputy Secretary of Defense Paul Wolfowitz, along with Under Secretary of Defense for Policy Douglas Feith and Vice President Cheney's Chief of Staff Scooter Libby, provide the full spectral dominance phrases for the mean and nasty Dick Cheney and sexy grandpa Donald Rumsfeld. Naked empire and corporate super-profits comprise the main elements in their worldview.

On the domestic side Attorney General John Ashcroft, once the extreme advocate of personal freedom and the states' rights wing of the Republican Party, now leads the charge against civil liberties and for prying into private affairs. The FBI, whose unique email system challenged any effort at direct communication with other agencies, now slips silently into other peoples' electronic and snail mail, taps their phones with skimpy cause, and surveils members of their family, just as it used to.

The security apparatus claims preeminence over all other state expenses. By routinely predicting terrorist acts, it keeps the citizens frightened and justifies its intrusion into business life as well. A vociferous states' righter and senator until 2001, Ashcroft now wants seemingly unlimited power for his federal agencies. He also favors a church-state marriage, outlawing of abortion, and denial of homosexuals' rights to marriage or marital benefits. Ashcroft, now the unofficial Commissar of Religious Activities, told a conservative Denver audience on January 13 that the government has discriminated against far-right religious groups, the upholders of national virtue, by not giving them taxpayers' money.

Budget-cutting conservatives ended up slashing social spending funds directed toward the poor. Supposedly to pursue terrorists and the axis of evil, Rummy and Dick encouraged the military brass and CIA to demand a $400 billion budget, far higher than any figure submitted during the cold war.

Is this charade saleable? Will the public accept a mounting defense budget at the expense of their jobs and Social Security without wondering whether it's for defense or world conquest?

Go back to the lesson of Vietnam. The US political and military classes understood that we shouldn't again fight anyone who could fight back. After 1975, when Congress cut off funds for the Vietnam War, President Ford attacked Cambodian vessels in supposed retaliation for the April 1975 seizure of a US merchant ship, the SS Mayaguez in international waters off the Cambodian coast.[2] In April 1980, Jimmy Carter later sent a mission to Iran to rescue the US hostages, but serious combat didn't erupt until 1983, when Reagan stood firmly transfixed by the Vietnam Syndrome. Serious Muslim enemies in Lebanon bombed a US Marine barracks and killed almost 200 men. Following the counsel of his wife Nancy's astrologer, he refused to send troops to Central America to defeat the leftist government of Nicaragua. US casualties would certainly have ensued. Instead, he unleashed the CIA and its Nicaraguan Contras against the Sandinistas. When he did pick military intervention spots, like Grenada on October 25, 1983, he insisted on an overkill number of US troops to defeat a nonexistent enemy.

It took time for the military and the White House to understand how to stage aggression against weak nations and spin it as heroism. "Panama George" (Bush 41) captured Panama Strong Man "Tough Tony" Noriega in 1989, after the spinners built up Noriega's forces as serious opposition. By demonizing Noriega, and exaggerating his strength, the White House fabulists could present Bush as a hard-hitting hero who had done irreparable damage to the drug trade. (The drug trade barely felt the Panama invasion, but fifty-two felons, convicted on drug charges, testified against Noriega at his Miami trial and subsequently received sentence reductions.)

Then, the White House simulated boxing promoter Don King and converted Saddam Hussein, a fiftieth-rated lightweight once in their corner, into a heavyweight contender who represented pure evil. In fact, Saddam had no defense against US power. The Gulf War should have been called a "technological massacre" rather than a war.

After Clinton's sporadic bombing of targets in Iraq, Sudan, and Afghanistan in 1998 followed by the former Yugoslavia in 1999, and his ambivalence toward conquering remote places all by ourselves, the reign of Boy George the Emperor began.

"Scale back," he said in his campaign, expressing an approach to foreign policy that coincided with his ignorance on the subject. Then came 9/11. The world changed and the naked imperialists and their plans emerged from their closets or Cabinets. Some, like the influential Perle, have shrouded their shadowy organizations in secrecy. Wow, they must be really important!

Within weeks Bush launched a "war against terrorism" and an "axis of evil." Subsequently, administration officials declared that they would engage in pre-emptive strikes and deploy nuclear weapons if necessary against their foes, like Iraq, which has no nukes and therefore merits no respect. Yet Bush can invade with probable impunity, maybe encounter some chemical and biological weapons.

North Korea took this rhetoric at face value. After Bush placed them and their loathed leader into the axis of evil club, the Koreans logically deduced that only having nuclear weapons could defend them. When North Korea revealed in early October 2002 that it might actually have a few nukes and that it would withdraw from the Nuclear Nonproliferation Treaty, thus imitating Bush's example of withdrawing from treaties, they won some respect. Although W personally hates North Korean leader Kim Jong Ill (W said he didn't like leaders who starve their people), he has agreed to talk with him, but not negotiate. For Bush, talking means offering the despised Kim oil and money in return for Korea's stopping nuclear weapons development. I'm trying to figure out what "negotiation" could mean.

I conclude this after sifting through countless articles and reports. But it's not easy to discern reality from the news sources. On January 15, I perused the MSN headlines looking for help in defining the difference between talking and negotiating with North Korea.

I learned that Nicole Kidman coped with her divorce by working out her emotional problems while making millions filming *The Hours*.

Equally important, Cameron Diaz had to miss the premieres of *Gangs of New York* in several European hot spots because of an outbreak of acne and Kate Winslett suffered the humiliation of getting her curves (read a trace of real human fat?) airbrushed out to make her look more beautiful (emaciated) in some *GQ* photos.

Further into the news, I discover that the White House spinsters (no relation to unmarried women) plan to virtually airbrush the fat that would go to the rich under Bush's tax plan. Under the guise of helping the little guy with a tax rebate, the plunderers have already begun filling their pockets while the naked imperialists under the umbrella of fighting terrorism have begun to conquer the world—and make hefty profits in the process: oil, weapons, rebuilding Iraq after the US bombs destroy it.

And few in Congress object loudly to the piratical agenda. The protestations from the Democratic leadership amounted to a wimpy plea to carry out aggression against Iraq with our allies, not alone, and a whine to spend a little money on social stuff. Then Senate Majority Leader Tom Daschle did fly into a rage, but only when he felt that Bush had impugned his and his colleagues' patriotism; he didn't care about innocent Iraqis or US GIs dying.

The rest of the public, the Rove gang hoped, would remain consumed with consuming and with the ever-growing pressures of surviving daily work and home life; as well as the idiosyncrasies and travails of actors, singers, and athletes.

"So," I told my now-more-frustrated student, "the Bush Administration defies traditional policy analysis. It displays symptoms of bipolar disorder in which the compulsion to pillage at home and the obsession to conquer abroad directs policy. To undergird such rapacious behavior, the controllers of policy in the White House have created the permanent insecurity state, which they disguise under the 'security' label, a far cry from *Peanuts*' thumb and blanket. Security today means taking off your shoes and undoing your belt at airports, undergoing wanding, and a variety of other meaningless procedures that supposedly will thwart the terrorists. Security means not knowing what the predictable, periodic yellow and orange alerts mean. If you're a Muslim or Arab-American, or just look like one, life has become anxiety-ridden. You can expect a police raid at any time. You can expect that Ashcroft will declare your charity a terrorist front and freeze its assets.

"The security state thrives on insecurity. Under the banners of urgency, federal police pry into your personal business. Security checks at borders have grown longer. Do people hesitate to go to crowded malls after Ashcroft declares an orange alert? This hurts business, a symptom of this bipolar criminal madness. Let's see if the security state can coexist with the shopping culture. If not, goodbye Bush—if he allows the votes to get counted this time."

November 2002

QUESTION FOR HOLLYWOOD SQUARES: *Can you wage a war on terrorism and simultaneously perfect and export democracy?*
ANSWER: *Yes, the film stars Bruce Willis as the man who leads hundreds of US soldiers to assassinate Saddam Hussein's sons and Jennifer Lopez as the woman who ratted on them and then teaches Iraqis the virtues of voting—because she's so sexy.*

How 9/11 Events Helped Democracy to Evolve toward Perfection

America exports Democracy big time, in the form of ideology.

(1) Hold elections like ours and you'll take a step toward political health or risk joining the axis of evil.
(2) Watch our entertainment like *Baywatch*, the finest quality T&A, old-time drama *Dallas*, and *Jerry Springer*, a combination of personal treachery and hilarious loss of dignity, and other exciting scenarios Hollywood produces.
(3) "Free market" capitalism works. Restrict our capital and export products and you'll get what's coming to you.

Americans take democracy for granted. We've overcome slavery, segregation (a few remnants remain in the Senate and Bohemian Grove,[3] perhaps), and all kinds of ethnic, racial, and gender biases. We're not perfect, but we're about as good as it gets.

We know bad guys like Saddam Hussein when we see them, and this makes us feel morally indignant. Indeed, some zealous believers have joined President Bush in his call for war against Iraq and maybe Islam in general. In this war, democracy can finally conquer Islamic fascism (not like the half-baked Crusades of centuries ago). Saddam the secular fascist or the Al Qaeda-Taliban-Wahhabi theocratic thugs, they're all haters of western civilization and therefore dangerous.

In light of some recent events, skeptics suggest, shouldn't we ask some questions about the substance of our democracy before aggressively promoting its export in all forms, especially military?

A quick review will indicate how our democracy has rapidly evolved in recent years even before 9/11. Go back to 2000, a year that made democratic history when less than a plurality of voters (about twenty-three percent of the eligible electorate) chose the president. The Supreme Court ruled that a republican form of government like ours didn't require vote counting to choose a president. So Bush won. I do not claim, as some bitter liberals do, that the Court's five Republicans simply out-voted the four Democrats out of partisan politics. The Court did count its own votes more precisely than those of Florida voters, but that's only natural.

In 2002, the Bush Administration further modified our system by replacing a slightly open government with that of an almost completely secret one. It's more efficient than having to account to Congress. The new administration tells Congress to stick its head in the toilet when it doesn't feel like sharing secrets of state. And Congress barely complains.

If this isn't development, it sure is growth (don't confuse this with tumors). In our "war against terrorism," the US government has had to license itself to execute people without trials, hearings, or other legal niceties. Some CIA officials apparently objected to this new wrinkle on the grounds that other nations could reciprocate. But their pleas went unheeded by the hardheaded realists. We only murder those we feel certain deserve it.

So, in November 2002, the US government dispatched via a drone-fired missile operated by the CIA an alleged Al Qaeda official in Yemen, identified as such by unidentified intelligence sources. A few others died in the car with him. The costs of the war on terrorism! To get one bad guy, you may have to kill five others. This evolution of democracy does have roots in our settling the wild west.

In addition, Bush has stretched the word "democracy" to make it compatible with concepts that purists once considered undemocratic. For example, the administration applied the term "enemy combatants" to include people that facts later showed were actual human beings who may not have had any connections to combat, the enemy, or terrorism. The December 22 *Los Angeles Times* reported that "The United States is holding dozens of prisoners at Guantánamo Bay who have no meaningful connection to Al Qaeda or the Taliban, and were sent to the maximum-security facility over the objections of intelligence officers in Afghanistan who had recommended them for release, according to military sources with direct knowledge of the matter."

When civil liberties lawyers tried to get them released or when judges objected to their incarceration without access to habeas corpus, government officials sneered because they knew—somehow—these men were hardened Al Qaeda terrorists. Well, some of them might have been! Okay, mistakes happen!

After more than a year of illegal detention, the *Times* found some "classified intelligence reports" that say that "dozens of the detainees are Afghan and Pakistani nationals" and who were "farmers, taxi drivers, cobblers, and laborers. Some were low-level fighters conscripted by the Taliban in the weeks before the collapse of the ruling Afghan regime."

"None of the 59 met U.S. screening criteria for determining which prisoners should be sent to Guantánamo Bay," military sources said.

"But all were transferred anyway, sources said, for reasons that continue to baffle and frustrate intelligence officers nearly a year after the first group of detainees arrived at the facility."

If intelligence officers feel frustrated, how does a typical citizen deal with the dramatic changes in our political life? Homeland Security has become another new feature added to American democracy in the twenty-first century. Once the domain of the armed forces, homeland security responsibility now rests on the shoulders of a new ministry, which bears its name. Previously, many people understood our democracy to include rigorous defense of human rights. But on December 19, Attorney General John Ashcroft modified that old-fashioned notion and ordered the arrest in Southern California of some 2500 men and boys who volunteered to register with the INS and get fingerprinted. But they volunteered, complained the civil libertarians. In democracy everyone knows that no good deed goes unpunished. These people paid for their blind trust in our system. Indeed, our democracy is based on hard-nosed realism!

After 9/11, Congress passed a "Patriot Act" to "protect us." The administration had presented them with classified material to show the immediacy of the threat and Congress acted obediently. It defied the wisdom of the late journalist I. F. Stone who said, "Never believe anything government officials say. They're all liars." George Jean Nathan called patriotism "the elevation of real estate above principles." Well, Bush understood that elevation means reaching greater heights of profit-making, so he included as patriotic the passing of a fast track for free trade in Latin America to help our wealthy investors make more money faster.

That's why the already wealthy investors invest more—into presidential campaign funds. Real power to dip into the public trough in our democracy has always belonged in the executive branch. The Administration buys lots of things and makes lots of contracts to get needed things done. Congress rewards its contributors through legislation, but the Administration gets to actually spend our tax money. Some call this looting the Treasury. But such talk besmirches our beloved Armed Forces, for example, which does a good share of the purchasing.

Indeed, Air Force lieutenant colonels order over $50 billion a year of military paraphernalia. Their job description says that they lead squadrons, but thanks to the productivity and flexibility of our democracy we have produced many times more officers of that rank than squadrons, so they buy instead of fly. Voicing opinions against new weapons systems, they learned, does not enhance their military or post-military careers, usually as vice president of a defense company in charge of selling its wares to the Pentagon. Now, that's a lesson in how the new American democracy actually works. "Be all that you can be," I believe the motto says. It means earn all you can earn, and never turn down a chance to make money the easy way.

Our electorate theoretically has a choice between voting for more weapons spending (not exactly defense because no country is attacking or plans to attack) or investing in health, education, environmental cleanup, or dealing with poverty. According to the March-April 2003 *Revolution, The Journal for RNs and Patient Advocacy*, some seventy-five million Americans lack access to medical care, tens of millions live in environmentally compromised areas, and millions live on the streets. President Reagan believed they preferred the streets, and many conservatives believe that government making health care available intrudes on peoples' personal choices.

So, issues related to helping poor people rarely appear in modern campaigns, lest they infringe on individual rights to love the outdoors or not see a doctor when sick. Those who raise these themes incite "class warfare" by harkening back to the New Deal of the 1930s and The Great Society of the mid-1960s. In those "unfree" times, according to modern conservatives, the government actually helped citizens, thereby making them lazy and spoiled. Thanks to the evolution of our democracy, however, only a minority of House and Senate Democrats continue to push for these outdated programs, and they have little hope of realizing them.

How ironic that polls show that the majority of Americans agree with what the Democrats offer. But they don't vote. In our democracy the "incompetent many" stayed home, or went to work and didn't have time to vote in the November 2002 congressional election. The "corrupt few," known as the elite, now manipulate the electoral system and continue to insist that the people voted for them. That's quite a trick, you'll have to admit. Most eligible voters were too preoccupied with more important issues or didn't find the candidates interesting enough to even dislike them. Those A-type millionaires who did vie for the few "contestable" congressional seats campaigned by placing very clever albeit negative and downright nasty spots on TV as their shortcut to dealing with "issues." Since they paid lots of money for these malicious slurs, one supposes that they pleased lots of viewers, especially those who have become hooked on shows like *Jerry Springer*. Where else could you see a grandmother proudly admitting on national television that she's getting it on with her granddaughter's twenty-one-year-old husband because "the little twit doesn't know how to satisfy a man like I do."

"If voting actually changed anything, they'd make it illegal," someone once remarked. The US government has added to that adage. When voters abroad made the "wrong" choice, the CIA in collaboration with the US-trained military had helped de-elect the candidate: Mohammed Mossadegh, overthrown in Iran in 1953; Jacobo Arbenz, ousted in Guatemala, 1954; Joao Goulart, removed in Brazil, 1964; and Salvador Allende, killed in Chile, 1973. Even though George Bush received less votes than Al Gore in 2000, neither the CIA nor the military used their power to block his ascent to the presidency, thanks to the brilliant intervention of our Supreme Court.

So, we embrace our peculiar democracy and offer it freely abroad to those who want it and those who don't. If only those Middle Easterners or old Fidel Castro in Cuba would dance to our political rhythms, they could experience the satisfaction of US-style elections. Think of the fun people could have watching millionaire Arabs or Cubans insulting each other on TV! If these "less blessed" peoples could grasp our optimal way of life, the US government could probably normalize relations with them—well, if they do exactly what it says.

Our pundits have modified the word democracy as it's used elsewhere with adjectives like "imperfect," "changing," "class-based," and "race-based," but barely anyone challenges the word itself in our great country. When bin Laden and his conniving minions tried to sow fear and thus force us to undo the protection for dissent, minority rights, and accountability in government, we showed him how we could quickly modify our political culture. Thanks to our agile leaders, we've adopted a balanced mixture of police state practices against resident aliens and dissenting citizens with continued tolerance for modest protest, provided it proves benign. Overseas, we have shown the efficacy of practicing raging disrespect for law, including authorizing murder; that's what constitutes democracy as 2002 comes to a close.

Those utopians, longing nostalgically for a return to the unfettered shopping mall-freeway culture of yesteryear, when "commerce *über alles*" was the only slogan of the day, will have to wait a long time. Security first and shopping second has become the rule under the US' post-national security state democracy. Americans have met Muslim fear and loathing with genuine democratic fear and loathing. The US government has bent its democratic principles to meet all contingencies. So, export away Señor Bush. Let the world feel US power. And don't forget the babes on *Baywatch*!

On March 19, 2003, George W. Bush ordered US forces to attack Iraq. Had some expert been monitoring the world's fragile legal equilibrium he would have detected a profound tremor. Bush's casus belli focused on Iraqi President Saddam Hussein's accumulation of biological, chemical, and nuclear weapons of mass destruction, his imminent threat to use them and or provide them to Al Qaeda terrorists with whom he allegedly had close ties. For those at home, the televised war resembled the regular television shows; for those at war, the chronically present cameras might have caused some confusion. Cameras recorded "heroic" rescues of women GIs, like Pvt. Jessica Lynch, with the dramatic[4] embellishments required by the grammar of the medium, TV, not war.

When the war ended, President Bush pushed further the merger between the virtual world of TV and the real world of politics.

Different Worlds

President George W. Bush's world revolves around images, winning political battles, and raising lots of money for election campaigns. The Chief Executive has little time to think about the vicissitudes of daily life for those not in his power world, such as the tens of thousands who lose their jobs each month due to the slumping US economy.

To add a new twist to his exciting and upbeat universe, on May 1 W staged a triumphant arrival on the USS Abraham Lincoln, which White House set designers moved some thirty miles off shore to make for a dramatic landing. His fighter jet squealed to a stop. Emerging in a military flight suit, he saluted the sailors on deck as if he were one of them, this man who had gone AWOL for over a year when he escaped the Vietnam War by enlisting in the Texas Air National Guard, but not showing up for duty.

The scene creators had staged a militarized US version of the Potemkin Village. The aircraft carrier deck with applauding men and women sailors replaced the happy eighteenth-century Russian villagers and focused the public's attention on the mighty leader's formal declaration: he had won a victory over yet another heavyweight contender for the world crown. By KOing first Afghanistan and now the potent Iraq with "minor" losses of US servicemen and women and all told a few hundred billion dollars spent he had spread "liberty" throughout the world. The docile US media filmed and recorded for TV and radio and printed his drivel as truth in the newspaper.

The next day, at an unemployment office in Los Angeles, the lines had grown noticeably longer. Less conspicuously, the newspapers reported that in March, when Bush invaded Iraq, some 8.8 million Americans found themselves out of work, more than at any time since 1991 when his daddy first invaded Iraq.

"I used to work for TWA and then American [Airlines] absorbed me," a former flight attendant said as she waited in the unemployment line. She received her pink slip along with thousands of other airline employees and tens of thousands of workers in other industries. "No more health plan, no more putting away money for retirement, or putting the kids through college," the forty-seven-year-old single mother said. Her fifteen- and seventeen-year-old kids "may have to start in one of those community colleges. I don't figure that any airline is doing hiring right now, especially for people my age."

Flush with international success, Bush swears to focus on the stumbling economy so that new jobs will emerge. His advisers keep a close eye on economic policy as they plan for the 2004 electoral campaign. They recall that Bush (41) lost the 1992 election despite astronomically high poll ratings following his 1991 Gulf War victory because the voters didn't trust him to run the economy.

Bush (43) has promised that his tax-cut plan will create new jobs. It is unclear what he plans to do about the old, lost jobs. Under his proposal the richest one percent of the country would receive hundreds of millions of dollars in "tax savings." Bush asserts with dogmatic certainty that the wealthy will convert this lucre into jobs.

Bush knows about conversions from his own life. His life renovations involved switching from the Episcopal to the Methodist Church, his wife's religion. Thanks to that concession to Laura, according to Bruce Wilkenson, author of the religious best seller *The Prayer of Jabez*, "the Lord is in front of him." Bush fights his war on terrorism, Wilkenson told Judy Kean of *USA Today* (March 14, 2002), by starting "each day in prayer on his knees before reading and studying the Bible."

The born-again Bush traces his passage from jerk to missionary to a 1985 conversation with the Rev. Billy Graham, which prompted him to quit drinking at age forty. The college prankster at Yale now experiences rapture which he tries to translate into words in his speeches and policies. "I would not be president today," he said, "if I hadn't stopped drinking seventeen years ago. And I could only do that with the grace of God."

"He doesn't know how to run an economy," said a middle-aged man in the unemployment line. He drove a school bus after losing his six-figure income job in marketing at a high-tech company. His take-home pay dropped to about $20,000. Now, with cuts of up to twenty percent in the California education budget, he has lost even the school bus job. He points to his twitching cheek. "Unemployment gave me this," he says.

Most of those in line looked away. Their symptoms may have been internal. A few talked about the president's speech. "Irrelevant," said a construction worker. "I was afraid I'd miss *Will and Grace*," a young woman chimed in. The beauty salon where she worked in a Los Angeles working-class area's strip mall closed down. "Just no business," she said. "Those that haven't lost their jobs are hanging on to their money because they're afraid they might lose them. So, they cut their own hair or have their friends do it for free."

Bush attributes his military success to his religion, of course. God blesses our wars and curses our enemies. W acts humble when talking about Jesus Christ and God, but becomes aggressive when promoting federal money for faith-based initiatives to run programs for the poor. His religious constituents, who worked as foot soldiers in his election campaign, must feel repaid. Congress has not yet approved this plan to cross the line between church and state. "Our governments must not fear faith," he exhorted Republicans at a Party fundraiser in Baltimore in March. "We must welcome faith in our society.'"

Faith does not put food on the family table, however. The drooping US economy translates into pain for millions of people. As Peg Tyre and Daniel McGinn report in the May 12 *Newsweek*, "a growing problem of 'underemployment' goes beyond the nation's 8.8 million jobless. Their numbers include people forced to accept part-time work, all those new-found 'consultants' who are playing computer solitaire but producing little income, and 'discouraged workers' who've given up job hunting altogether."

Protestant fundamentalism would have us understand the world as the working out of biblical scenarios. Thus the far-right wing in religion and politics remains unconcerned with earthly phenomena such as global warming or melting polar ice caps. If we're witnessing the battles of Gog and Magog (in the Middle East) that precede Armageddon, who cares about beached whales? The day of Reckoning is upon us, anti-Semitic preachers scream as they rouse their flock to support the state of Israel, even though God doesn't hear the prayers of the Jewish population of that state.

Biblical scenarios amidst high technology baffle me. The Messiah's imminent arrival is accompanied by a loss of humor. In Jewish lore a fellow tells his wife he took a job for ten shekels a month to wait outside the village gate to welcome the Messiah when he arrives. His wife berates him for accepting such low wages. "Well," he explains, "I'm guaranteed long-term job security."

The day after Bush's speech I repeat the joke to teenagers visiting my teenager. I talk about unemployment and California's deficit. They don't laugh when I say that Bush has completed "the disarmature of Iraq." They work or play at conquering a video game.

None of them evince interest in born-again religion, the president's tax plan, or his speech on the USS Abraham Lincoln. Have I discovered yet another American world, the one Oscar Levant may have referred to when he explained why people didn't understand Los Angeles? "They see only the superficial layer of tinsel," he said. "Underneath that lies the real tinsel."

May 2003

Shiite Happens

For bureaucratic reasons, we settled on one issue, weapons of mass destruction (as justification for invading Iraq) because it was the one reason everyone could agree on.
—Paul Wolfowitz to *Vanity Fair* reporter, May 9, 2003

Can both fresh water and salt water flow from the same spring?
—The Bible on lies, James 3:11 NIV

Having fibbed his way into a war with a virtually disarmed and weak enemy, Bush now gloats over *his* victory. Acting as if he understood his grandiose albeit vague statements about historic alliances, W held forth in old and new Europe before going to Egypt to "make peace in the Middle East."

The new empire visits the old world. After 9/11, Washington demanded that its junior partners simply rubberstamp Bush's plans, like making war against Iraq. This placed a level of unprecedented stress on the formal and informal alliances that emerged from World War II and from the post-Soviet era.

For example, most of the partners except the British, Australians, Poles, and a few lesser powers, asked for a just cause to back such a war. "Saddam Hussein is evil," Bush first explained.

"And?" they responded.

Blair and Bush then stared pointedly at their intelligence chiefs.

And, poof, the intelligence agencies delivered reasons.

Then the media, Congress, and the United Nations began to debate them as axioms: should we disarm Saddam with or without war?

Documents from Africa, Bush claimed, proved Saddam had a nuclear capacity. The US and British governments claimed further proof by citing dissident Iraqi "experts," who affirmed Saddam's biological and chemical weapons programs.

The nuclear documents turned out to be forgeries, the exiled Iraqis had not said what US officials claimed, and neither Bush nor Blair had hard evidence of Saddam constituting an imminent threat to "security."

In March 2003, Bush declared that the UN inspectors, who had found nothing, had diddled long enough. The time had come for war to disarm Hussein. It took the Americans more time to conquer Iraq than it did the Germans to defeat Poland at the onset of World War II. And the Poles fought back!

Now Bush has switched roles from conquering hero to world statesman, and commander of the US colonial government in Iraq.

In this role, he has had little to celebrate. The June 1 *Los Angeles Times* reported three Americans died in a vehicle accident in Iraq and in another road mishap, and a US supply truck ran over and killed a three-year-old Iraqi child. During the course of the week, the US military occupation command reported several incidents of Iraqis firing at and killing US soldiers. "US troops are afraid to go out at night," reported Robert Fisk in the May 31 *Independent*.

Just another week of routine colonial occupation, a tradition sorely lacking in US history unless, of course, one includes Indian and Mexican territory.

But as Bush insisted on the urgency of Middle East peace, the media still referred to George Washington Bush, not quite the president who never told a lie.

Iraqis ignore such nonsense. They compare their current plight under colonial occupation with Saddam's dictatorship. One Arab on a May 31 news report on World Link TV said, "Saddam was bad, but we had water and electricity." Indeed, Saddam's gang had both systems operating after Coalition bombs destroyed the water and electrical generating systems during Gulf War I.

The fact that most Iraqi soldiers and civilians didn't fight means that they don't think of themselves as a defeated people who must abide by the rule of the winners, especially the British, who had occupied Iraq in previous colonial incarnations. But when looting broke out, the liberating GIs stood by. Indeed, for weeks the Americans did not fashion a constabulary and Iraqis got truly pissed off.

As the intense summer heat descends on much of the country, the threat of disease looms heavily. A May 21, 2003 UN Daily Briefing reported that damage from fighting and the persistent looting have rendered the Al Rustumia sewage plant inoperable, resulting in one million tons of raw sewage discharged daily into the Tigris and Dayala Rivers.

Government barely exists and now hundreds of thousands of Iraqi soldiers, recently demobilized and thrown out of jobs, further complicate the task of colonial administrator L. Paul Bremer.

At the time of this writing, Iraqi soldiers in Basra demanded that the British occupiers pay them. Other soldiers in different cities threatened violence if the Americans didn't meet their demands. Mark Kingwell, writing in the May 28 *National Post*, quotes one Arab, "The Americans promised us food and medicine and freedom. But we have lost our homes, our land, our crops.... If we don't have a solution, we will fight the Americans even if they kill us. It is better than sitting here with nothing and just dying."

Patrick Cockburn wrote in the May 30 *Independent* that "all this military triumphalism ignored the disastrous reality of post-war Iraq." Although Iraqis generally hated Saddam, they have not taken to the United States and Britain either. If the occupying powers "are going to stay, they are going to have to fight."

In the nineteenth century Americans discovered that it was easier to kill Indians than govern them. Will we successfully apply colonial rule to Iraq when we never could in our own country, the Philippines, or Puerto Rico? Yet, before the war even began, the ahistorical President Bush held forth a utopian reconstruction plan for Iraq.

This was the very president who had attacked nation-building ideas as utopian when he campaigned in 2000. But formal empire carries burdens. The brilliance of past US empire consisted precisely in its informality. The US controls where it counts, in the economy and military, and lets the natives rule themselves as long as they remain obedient.

This method has allowed the United States to remain free from the costly and embarrassing burdens born by the older empires of Europe. It even allowed the United States to declare its interest in upholding international law since it has traditionally used covert ops to overthrow disobedient governments.

Iraq has changed that long and successful trajectory. The world now sees through the transparent rhetoric, as Kingwell observes, that the United States "dresses up self-interest as universal benefit."

As some colleagues rejoiced in the TV images of Iraqi freedom, I shrugged and said that we had witnessed that the United States military could easily defeat a disarmed third-world country. Now watch and see the very Republican Bechtel and Halliburton Corporations make quick profits rebuilding what our Air Force needlessly destroyed.

Air power destroyed Iraq, but can't run the place after conquest. The Iraqis are not cooperating with the vague US plans to "democratize" the entire region (a word that translates to the people of the area as shopping malls, Disneyland, and elections in which candidates insult each other on TV and don't talk about the issues).

Instead of western democracy, "Shiite happens" as one e-mail said, referring to the impending change from the once-secular Iraqi society to one in which religious police have emerged in the form of committees to prevent vice and to promote virtue, *à la* Iran during the Ayatollah.

"Doing good" in the world has provided US foreign policy with a highly successful veneer for informal imperialism. As Iraq descends into chaos and ethnic fighting, Bush confidently asserts that his plan for a US-style Middle East will begin to unfold. The world's greatest empire still hidden from the American public has started to remake ancient societies in its image. It does so behind the veneer of its war against terrorism. It does so as long as the US public remains distracted and disconnected from its own interests and history.

Our leaders have flaunted John Quincy Adams' July 4, 1821 warning to not seek "foreign monsters." Hey, how do you justify a $400 billion military budget without having at least one foreign monster? The Bushies took the nation into war by exaggerating the threat of the Saddam monster. Now they count on national memory to focus only on the victory of the US Armed Forces in Iraq while filtering out their lies about the causes of the war. *Veni, vidi, vici* and all of that old Americana!

June 2003

The Quiet American Returns on Film

FOWLER: You and your like are trying to make a war with the help of
    people who just aren't interested.
PYLE: They don't want communism.
FOWLER: They want enough rice. They don't want to be shot at. They
    want one day to be much the same as another. They don't want our
    white skins around telling them what they want.
                     —Graham Greene, *The Quiet American*

I saw the movie version of Graham Greene's novel just before Miramax
film exec Harvey Weinstein quietly, and temporarily, yanked *The Quiet
American* from the market, despite the good reviews it had gleaned. The
word around the Hollywood industry had it that given the current climate, the strains of "anti-Americanism" in the film might offend sensitive
publics, especially those in high government posts.

Just as during the post-World War II witch hunt, the government
established the informal post-9/11 rules and the Hollywood studio
moguls enforced them. The FBI did not circulate to Hollywood a memo
saying, "Don't portray American officials as terrorists." Indeed, tacit
standards of "acceptability" meant that the business heavies didn't need
to send out a "Don't circulate critical films" memo to producers. The FBI
did circulate to the airlines a "no-fly list" of antiwar activists whose
names appear on airline computer screens as "undesirables." After 9/11,
the FBI also circulated a list to large corporations of people it "suspected" of having "possible" terrorist links, mostly Muslim-Americans,
of course.[5]

So, the government didn't have to intimidate Miramax executives
overtly, who had already heard about new categories such as "enemy
combatants," those without rights, and authorization for the CIA to
assassinate "terrorists." Hollywood execs knew that the new government
lists coincided with the denial of old individual rights, especially those
connected with privacy.

Hollywood responds viscerally when the government restricts liberties
and widens its intrusive powers. The latest James Bond movie, *Die
Another Day*, reinforces the government's version of recent history by

making terrorist allies out of North Korea and Cuba. But Washington's message goes beyond simple ideological obedience. After 9/11/01, Americans have effectively lost not only their innocence but their tolerance for naysayers as well. CEOs get nervous when their relations with the government become less than harmonious. Pro-American pictures are in; anything remotely resembling critical positions on the red, white, and blue is taboo.

The company had held a test screening of *The Quiet American* in New Jersey on September 10, 2001. The audience liked the film. The next day, September 11, world reality changed. So Miramax' subsequent "tests" showed that audiences supposedly found the film's implicit critique of US policy less than appealing. Predictably, some flunky PR man denied that Miramax delayed the release plans and then removed the film quickly from the market because of 9/11 reverberations. You judge for yourself.

Under the new post-9/11 official script, we as a nation lost almost 3000 lives to the "cowardly" bombers, and our collective virginity to boot. To remedy this, we would have to stand together against the terrorists, whatever that means. Bush launched a "promote America as the virtuous" campaign. Let's not hear any negatives about our wonderful way of life. Long Live Disneyland and the Super Bowl! Shop, fellow Americans, and show those Al Qaeda nasties what we really stand for.

Abroad, Bush took it to the adversaries. No more Mr. Nice Guy. It's time to show a knuckle to those ungrateful foreigners. So, instead of learning meaningful lessons as a result of the fiendish attack of 9/11, like understanding why they did it and how Americans can deal with the causes of this terrorism, Bush and his ideologues opportunistically embarked on the next real-life chapter of *The Quiet American*. In *The Quiet American Returns*, Sylvester Stallone can show us how assassinating large numbers of suspected Al Qaeda operatives can earn the love of an Arab beauty and the gratitude of the western world, and he can be quiet, that is, not speak much during the film.

The sequel could suggest an implicit Hollywood-style answer to the questions, "Why do they hate us" or "How come anti-Americanism runs rampant in the Arab world?" Stallone, able to take on hundreds of armed killers and dispatch all of them, virtually shows them that we're superior, certainly at killing and hamming for the camera. Since we're Americans, as Hollywood films imply, everyone knows we're inherently virtuous. We saved Afghanistan, suffered a few casualties from friendly fire, killed only a few thousand innocent civilians, and took a major step toward confronting the axis of evil. We shall become missionaries again and destroy more nations in order to save them. Hey, the price for freedom!

Perhaps future historians will label this era the Noisy American Period. They may even conclude that Osama bin Laden wrote the outline for the script in this latest saga of US imperial history. With Vietnam almost three decades behind us—out of memory for most Americans— we see characters similar to those who told us that our holy mission was to fight communism in Vietnam and bring democracy to that far-off land. Indeed, some of those very people now do lucrative business with the communist government of Vietnam. In the new era of bullying, boasting, cockiness, and self-righteousness, the horrible results of our decade-plus military involvement in Vietnam have faded from historical memory. That conflict, my students assure me, occurred some time after the Greco-Roman era, but what does it have to do with today and terrorism?

Graham Greene warned us in the early 1950s when he wrote his insightful novel. In 1953, despite US military aid, the French were losing the war to retain control of Vietnam. As the communist government of the North won battle after battle, US officials began to plan their intervention. This is the setting for Thomas Fowler (Michael Caine) as Graham Greene's reporter covering this one of several anticolonial revolts, as adapted for the cinema by Australian director Philip Noyce. Fowler, in full middle age, lives with his young Vietnamese lover Phuong (Hai Yen Do). He meets a recently arrived US official attached to the Economic Aid Mission. Fowler senses that this overly sincere young man Alden Pyle (Brendan Fraser) will disturb his established order. It happens rapidly as Pyle falls instantly in love with the Vietnamese paramour. She symbolizes innocence, because he does not know better, and, of course, she represents a challenge.

Fowler realizes that his apparent political or philosophical differences with the young zealot always reading about making democracy go beyond the world of ideas. The Quiet American turns out to be not just a killer, but the quintessential terrorist. He makes his big bang in Saigon by planting bombs (the means) to bring democracy (the ends) and thus stave off the communist menace and transform Vietnam into a US-style nation. If one doubts the reality about Americans having this intensity of belief in our ability to export our order everywhere, read our more passionate op-ed writers today who have recently discovered the cause of the Iraqi people and extol our government to go to war to "liberate" them.

Ironically, Greene's book, written in the early 1950s, eerily predicted what the United States would do in Vietnam. The fictional Quiet American multiplied. Thousands of these zealots became real protagonists in one of the bloodiest wars of the late twentieth century. Always in the name of spreading democracy to Vietnam, the Quiet Americans advocated ever more mass bombing of Vietnamese cities, dropping of napalm on its villages and people, and the destruction of its vegetation through the application of Agent Orange. The Quiet American was epitomized by the young US officer in the late 1960s who lamented to a reporter in all innocence that "We had to destroy the village in order to save it."

Those men, like Greene's Alden Pyle, get their *esprit de corps* from the intellectuals whom we read in the newspaper and magazine columns, such as the octogenarian William Safire and the know-it-all-but-doesn't-like-to-fight-personally Thomas Friedman of the *New York Times*. These chickenhawks eschew the lesson that Graham taught fifty years ago. The failure in Vietnam taught them nothing about the impossibility of exporting our order to Afghanistan, Iraq, Iran, North Korea, or, well, you pick it. These missionary writers do not, of course, do the fighting. They also glide over some of the issues that make the constant repetition of the word "democracy" ring hollow.

Do they not realize that the USA is a country where the majority doesn't vote, where the majority of federal offices are uncontested? They want to spread this abroad? What none of them advocate, however, is the distinguishing fact that makes us special: immense and badly distributed wealth.

Fowler, Greene's British protagonist, the antithesis of those Americans who try to "win the hearts and minds" of the natives, goes native. He smokes opium in the colonial tradition and also takes his pleasures from the young Vietnamese woman on whom he has become dependent emotionally. She prepares his pipe and gives him pleasures. She demands little. He loves her. What she feels for him remains enigmatic. Her money-grubbing sister plays a large role in the younger woman's affairs, but Phuong herself never stoops to such vulgarity. She maintains a façade of innocence, which makes her so attractive to both men. Ah, to be above the struggle, delicate and sensual, dignified and mysterious!

The Quiet American, intent on changing Vietnam, must also change relationships. But he has rules for both processes: taking the Vietnamese beauty from Fowler and forging his democratic third way between European colonialism and communism. Greene, the moral observer and critic, asks implicitly in the book what winning means in such a context. The American's less than superficial understanding of Vietnamese culture and history can only lead him and his nation to disaster. Is this why the film seems threatening now, when we're about to embark on yet another crusade in Iraq, to change the destiny of yet another country whose 5000 year old history and culture we do not understand?

Since the Puritans of Massachusetts Bay Colony, missionary zeal has led some Americans to spread "our way of life." But the Baal of shopping has replaced the angry Puritan God. The modesty and humility our ancestors assumed before the power of God has changed into bragging about "how great our country is," while Americans pop pills for stress of various kinds. Those across the world who have yet to hear or see the revealed word or image, will find in the new Quiet Americans a set of political missionaries who perpetrate the myth that "we" can export our almost perfect order. American misdeeds, like the fraud in the 2000 election, they attribute to aberrations.

Hollywood has exported the American ideal in movies and TV shows. It sells foreigners on an excellent police force, which has yet to find the anthrax killer, on superb doctors, who operate under corporate HMOs that exclude about seventy-five million people from health care, or clever lawyers who assure a fair trial for all their clients. How come in real life the rich white killers and thieves almost always get off or short sentences and the poor felons of color get life or death sentences?

Greene's Alden Pyle, a CIA heavy using a humanitarian cover, set out to liberate Vietnam by all means necessary. Liberation later meant "Rolling Thunder," the carpet-bombing of cities. Indeed, by 1973, US planes had dropped three times as many bombs on Vietnam as all the protagonists had used in World War II. Liberation meant destruction of Vietnamese cities and the deaths of some two million civilians. To free Vietnam from the yoke of communism meant destroying their rice fields with poisons and bombing their dikes, pouring millions of gallons of dioxin-laden Agent Orange on the countryside. The long-term effects of these "saving" devices used during war continue to haunt present generations. The United States destroyed infrastructure—as it did in Iraq in 1991—and massacred civilians. These were war objectives, not "collateral damage."

The American in the movie radiates sincerity, but his feelings for the young Vietnamese woman border on compulsive. Fowler notes this, but Pyle's very intensity makes him interesting. He is the moderate Fowler's antithesis. Then, in an action scene he saves Fowler's life. Fowler discovers later that the killers were Pyle's charges, the very "third force" he had bragged about. Under a façade of innocence and certainty, Pyle contains within himself all the seeds of a modern war criminal, a killer who "knows" that the future he helps usher in will more than atone for the deaths and damage he causes in the present. Fowler finally understands that Pyle is a terrorist, a man unable to see past his anti-communist ardor. He will destroy in the name of his cause. How is he different in character than the arch-fiends who did the 9/11 deeds?

Is this why the government doesn't want people to see *The Quiet American*? In 1947, Washington leaned on Hollywood executives to change their standards on hiring stars, directors, and writers and to change movie themes that might conceivably have connections with "Reds." This taboo included material that smacked of anti-Americanism. Having finished with the war against fascism, we were entering a new war against communism.

In 2002, having long finished with the commie menace, we've turned our attention to terrorism, the buzzword of our era. Terrorism means what we say: violence done to or planned against our country, not violence done by us or our allies to their enemies. For example, James Bond can blow to smithereens any number of bad North Koreans, because he is good and thus can practice pre-emptive violence. The applauding audience revels in his virtual pyrogenics.

The Quiet American goes beyond Vietnam. It describes American imperialism on the ground and portrays a modern imperialist. The over-confident Americans like Alden Pyle have pushed their "democracy" or "anti-communism" into killing fields in Iran, Guatemala, Chile, Colombia, and Indonesia, the list grows long. They had no interest in understanding Vietnamese nationalism albeit they read a few books about its culture and history. Today, they have no better understanding of similar forces in the Arab world. They make moral judgments about our systemic superiority and then reaffirm them by reciting Christian and democratic clichés.

Watch the texture of the film and the movement of the Vietnamese actors and learn lessons about Vietnam's aesthetics. Listen to Fowler's lines and understand true conservatism. Responding to Pyle's rationalization for war, Fowler says, "Isms and ocracies. Give me the facts." This statement should reverberate through the political chambers. Like Pyle in *The Quiet American*, Bush has mastered the art of unsupported allegations.

Yet American aesthetics link truth with virtue. It is unlikely that Bush considered Aristotle's other linkage, between the beautiful and the good, before he ordered troops into Iraq with his current "liberation" mission. In Vietnam, the exotic tropical humidity does not dictate the ways of life, but the desert does.[6]

Revised: January 2004

Shopping, the End of the World, and G.W. Bush: Part I

In my neighborhood of trimmed lawns and two or more car garages, with one or two additional vehicles parked outside the garage, I counted fifteen American flags in less than five minutes of my slow trot, most of them unfurled since the United States invaded Iraq in March 2003. One house had a sign with a US flag waving over a map of Iraq. Americans learn geography through war, experience the traumas of battle—well, virtually—and root for the good guys. We know we're good because God blesses America and fucks our enemies, with the help of the missiles, bombs, tanks, and other war technology with which He has blessed us. Our God loves peace and keeps us, as Gore Vidal quipped, in "perpetual war." Our God does not like opposition, from within, or from our former friends abroad. He has told our leaders, all of whom remain in close contact with Him, to punish such heretic behavior.

Our God is one of love and compassion, although he seems to act out of rage and retribution. But some of the media, particularly Fox and CNN, seem to have found hidden in FCC regulations some clause that dictates that news reporting means obeying the orders of our God-chosen political leaders, since the majority did not choose them. Former officers, like Lt. Col. Oliver North who, in violation of the law, conspired to sell missiles to Iran in the 1980s in order to fund the Nicaraguan Contras, now appear as honored war experts and cheerleaders for our troops.

On April 6, before I jogged through my neighborhood, I watched TV images of bombs and artillery shells decimating Iraq, Iraqi women and children pleading for water. One scene even showed a full hospital without running water, so the doctor could not mix plaster with which to make a cast for a small boy's broken arm.

Online I saw more horrific images from non-US sources, including *Agence France Presse*. Mutilated bodies of children and weeping adults holding their dead kids! Liberating Iraq! Yes, death is the ultimate liberation!

Bush has set forth "a worldview that is intrinsically paranoid," writes philosopher Francois Bernard in the March 31 *Ha'aretz*, "imbued with visions of the most regressive Crusades, drenched in a frightening symbolism that sees any external opposition as evidence of crime and in which every decision and every action bear the seal of a vengeful divinity." Since 9/11/01 (was this the work of the Devil?) God has emerged as the dominant force in US politics. This God preaches democracy, although its meaning has yet to become clear. It has something to do with good, the United States, the United Kingdom, and other members of the coalition of the willing, versus the axes of evil and their tacit partners in malice.

Our God teaches us that shopping and going to Disneyland constitute the highest spiritual values, outside of attending church once a week. Our God has singled us out among all peoples, even though we came from all peoples, as His chosen elite to reside in His promised land.

Well-dressed people pour out of churches, get in their SUVs, and drive to their $400,000-plus homes. Some will watch sports on TV, others will tune in to the presstitutes, as Uri Avnery calls them, who report on the war in Iraq. "Their original sin," he says,

> was their agreement to be 'embedded' in army units....A journalist who lies down in the bed of an army unit becomes a voluntary slave. He is attached to the commander's staff, led to the places the commander is interested in, sees what the commander wants him or her to see, is turned away from the places the commander does not want him to see, and does not hear what the army does not want him to hear. He is worse than an official army spokesman, because he pretends to be an independent reporter. The problem is not that he only sees a small piece of the grand mosaic of the war, but that he transmits a mendacious view of that piece.

The rosy reports on the "news" of the virtuous coalition troops' steady triumph over the unfair-fighting forces of evil give several residents of my suburban neighborhood reason to feel righteous, if not downright pious in their support of the Bush Administration's policy. Those Bush supporters I have spoken to see no relationship between their comfortable lifestyles and the devastation the US military has inflicted in Iraq. "Now we're even, for what they did to us," said a sales manager at a local hotel chain. He referred to 9/11, as if Saddam Hussein and the Iraqis had actually done those foul deeds. "They're not going to try that one again," he said smugly. Almost half of Americans polled blame Saddam for 9/11—thanks to President Bush's constant references to his "links" to terrorists, reported without critical comment by the media.

Most Americans don't have access through TV news or the daily print press of critical reporting coming out of Iraq. On April 8, Robert Fisk of the *Independent* filed this report.

> It looks very neat on television, the American marines on the banks of the Tigris, the all-so-funny visit to the presidential palace, the videotape of Saddam Hussein's golden loo. But the innocent are bleeding and screaming with pain to bring us our exciting television pictures and to provide Messrs Bush and Blair with their boastful talk of victory. I watched two-and-a-half-year-old Ali Najour lying in agony on the bed, his clothes soaked with blood, a tube through his nose....

Ignorant of and therefore oblivious to Iraqi pain, one would think the suburbanites would at least respond to their state's fiscal crisis. How much will they have to pay if Bush actually tries to realize his post-war reconstruction plans for Iraq? Californians, already faced with a $38 billion (and rising) state deficit, look forward to paying heavier state and local taxes to make up for the shortfall from the federal government's yearly allocation to the states. They do not seem to worry about additional costs for rebuilding Iraq. When I mention the tax cut for the very wealthy, their eyes glaze over.

I have also met the programmed "born-agains," those who believe robotlike that what they view on TV as current history is the working out of biblical prophecy. One woman mentioned the battles of Gog and Magog that must precede the final reckoning. She identifies "100 percent with our president." He, unlike the lascivious Bill Clinton, "is a true Christian." Most of the neighbors with whom I spoke said that the bloodshed had upset them, but "that's the price we have to pay for security," one man said as he pruned his roses.

In Iraq, the born-again Christians work with the US military. Meg Laughlin in the April 5 *Miami Herald* quoted Evangelical Christian Army Chaplain Josh Llano. "They want water. I have it, as long as they agree to get baptized," he said. "In so many ways," writes Laughlin, "this represents the true mindset of the individuals who have pushed this war. It is right down the line with the actions of this administration over the past three years; recall that, when our airmen were being held in China back in 2001, Mr. Bush was only concerned with whether or not they had Bibles."

Nothing in the fundamentalist theology seems to inhibit consumption, however. These God-fearing people buy gas-guzzling vehicles, pay Mexicans to mow their lawns and drop chemicals into their swimming pools, and take periodic vacations in Las Vegas—where God does not always bless them. In church, they listen to the pious sermons about what being a Christian means in daily life. But their interpretation of the Bible does not sensitize them to the pain of the Iraqis. I notice a satisfied, almost smug smile on the faces of the men as they announce their support for the president and his warlike policies. They repeat Bush's lines about the need to get rid of Saddam's "weapons of mass destruction" and "we had to act because the UN is worthless" arguments.

My neighbors have problems, like all people. Their suburban-reared kids often drink and then drive, use drugs and get caught, or fail to make college-level grades. But many of the parents themselves also tend to use addictive substances and then go into religious programs to recover, or get divorced, go bankrupt, and even commit suicide. Those I spoke with consider themselves good people, kind, charitable. Like many suburban families, my neighbors spend parts of their weekends on shopping expeditions for lawn, garden, patio and pool supplies, home furniture, kitchen needs, and, of course, clothing. Most of them cannot quite understand why some people would protest a war against a brute like Saddam Hussein in Iraq.

"Those hedonistic terrorists are getting what they deserve," opined one older neighbor with a prominently displayed flag on her lawn. She had just returned from her Baptist church service where she prayed for President Bush to prevail. Later she will take advantage of a sale to buy her grandchildren some new backpacks, for school books. "Lord knows, they sure get plenty of use." I nod. She says, "God bless you!"

In Iraq, Saddam invokes God as well. He continues to call on his people to resist in the name of the Muslim homeland and Allah. That God has lost this war. Or maybe just this battle for Iraq in the last days of born-again history?

April 2003

Part II

There shall be a fourth kingdom on earth that shall be different from all the other kingdoms; it shall devour the whole earth, and trample it down, and break it to pieces.

—Daniel 23

As I browsed the *New York Times* for news of Iraq, SARS, and the latest environmental disaster, my teenage daughter and her friends arrived with the nutritional equivalent of ecological bio-terrorism. They opened Burger King bags and unveiled massive cheeseburgers and grease-dripping Freedom fries (the French might refuse to have their name connected to such items), which they dunked into what Ronald Reagan once called a vegetable (ketchup). They drowned this cholesterol feast with noisy slurps from twenty-two ounce plastic Coke containers.

As they slowly sucked in the artery-clogging fast food and lounged on the sofa to watch reality TV, I recalled the messianic words from the Prince of Darkness, Richard Perle, "This is total war. We are fighting a variety of enemies. There are lots of them out there," he told John Pilger in the *New Statesman*, December 16, 2002. "If we just let our vision of the world go forth, and we embrace it entirely, and we don't try to piece together clever diplomacy but just wage a total war, our children will sing great songs about us years from now."

"If kids eat food like this," I thought, "the only songs they'll sing in the future will be hymns at each others' premature funerals." Can one encompass epic concepts such as waging perpetual war for perpetual peace on the one hand and harmonize them with a vision of a trivialized society whose spiritual glue is perpetual shopping and eating fast food?

The Bushies address this issue obliquely through religion, not political philosophy. For example, their policy planners reject the very premise of scientists' prognosis of disasters that will ensue from global warming. Indeed, neither corporate CEOs (except for insurance chiefs) nor government heavies seem to factor the global environment into their plans. The issue, instead, seems to be: how to divert public attention from environmental horror.

The May 7, 2003 *LA Times* reported, for example, that

> lawyers representing some 30,000 impoverished Ecuadoreans are expected to sue Chevron Texaco Corp. today, accusing the second-largest U.S. oil company of contaminating the rainforest and sickening local residents. The suit alleges that a Chevron Texaco unit discharged billions of gallons of contaminated water, causing widespread pollution and illness.

Other oil companies used similar practices in Nigeria. In 1999 Shell Oil injected a million liters of waste into an abandoned oil well in Erobie in the Niger Delta. Those who ate the crops or drank water in the area fell ill. Almost one hundred people died from poisonous amounts of lead, mercury, and other toxins. In 2001, exploration for new wells in Nigeria by western oil companies contaminated the fresh water supply, causing serious illness among the local population. The typical oil company response to such mishaps: "Hey, people drive cars; cars need gas; we supply the gas." Neither oil company CEOs nor the president addressed the medium- or long-term implications of using more fossil fuels.

When pushed, one corporate executive alluded to "God's will." At the 1997 Kyoto Conference on the environment, Jeremy Leggett, who wrote *The Carbon War: Global Warming and the End of the Oil Era* (2001), cornered Ford Motor Company executive John Schiller.

Leggett, a Greenpeacer, asked Schiller how he dealt with "a billion cars intent on burning all the oil and gas available on the planet." Schiller first denied that "fossil fuels have been sequestered underground for eons." He claimed, instead, that the Earth is just 10,000, not 4.5 billion years old, the age widely accepted by scientists. Schiller then referred Leggett to The Book of Daniel: "The more I look, the more it is just as it says in the Bible." In other words, Schiller's "theological" interpretation of the world foresees "earthly devastation [that] will mark the 'End Time' and return of Christ."

So, like the powerful people in the White House, just refer to biblical passages to explain those photos of melting ice caps on the Andes and Mt. Kilimanjaro and breakups of polar ice caps. Use Scripture to calm those excited by the warming effects of the now-frequent El Niños, which have a devastating impact on the sea and land's well-being.

I juxtapose my own fears over the deteriorating environment with the rapture experienced over such ecological decay by the very people who manage the destruction. They view optimistically the dire environmental warnings as sure signs that the end is near and the Messiah will return. As a kid in Hebrew school I learned that the Messiah would supposedly arrive and take all the Jews to Israel. When my father told my mother about this imminent event, she wailed in despair, "Just after we spent all that money fixing up the house?"

In the no-laughs born-again world, however, the Millennium means that the Lord will welcome a smog-filled planet so He can redesign it in His original Edenic form. Somehow He will afford to the true believers the necessary lungpower to survive and live for a thousand years in Nirvana.

If this sounds bizarre, then read Joan Bokaer, who studied the fundamentalists at the Center for Religion, Ethics, and Social Policy at Cornell University. Tens of millions of Americans, she reports, have taken up this apocalyptic form of religion. Not all of them shape their lives dogmatically around this religious vision, but they do tend to dismiss environmentalists as worrywarts.

Bokaer adds that these serious soldiers of God see their role as paving the pious road for the Lord's return. Like the Puritans who settled Massachusetts Bay Colony in the seventeenth century, these modern zealots predict Christ's return only at such a time when they have successfully carried out His work: purged the country of sinners and replaced the corrupt civil law with the dictates of the Bible, which includes, in foreign policy, promoting the battle of Armageddon by supporting Israel.

Like the seventeenth-century Puritans, they do not believe in the separation of church and state. The Puritans, however, studied science, believing that God had placed the challenge of discovery before them. Modern fundamentalists tend to disparage the discipline of research to learn about God's ways and instead direct their energies to promoting ultra-right politics: including belittling environmental concerns, supporting gun ownership and prayer in school, and outlawing abortion, along with supporting Israel, of course. So, long live Israel (even with its population of Jews, whose prayers God doesn't hear); hooray for depleted uranium in military shells and bombs.

This religious vision, or nightmare, strangely coincides with a blatantly consumerist society. The born-again president stands also for mainstream culture. George Bush's inflexibility of thinking, his dogmatic use of good and evil as politically defining poles, allows him to live with or ignore the obvious discrepancies and contradictions in his epic plan for world domination on the one hand and his trivial proclivity for destructiveness. "We need an energy bill that encourages consumption," he told a Trenton, NJ audience on September 23, 2002. "Sure," I say to myself, "wait till one billion Chinese and one billion Indians all drive SUVs."

In the October 11, 2002 *Counterpunch*, Katherine van Wormer cites brain studies to "reinforce what recovering alcoholics and their counselors have been saying for years; long-term alcohol and other drug use changes the chemistry of the brain. These anomalies in brain patterns are associated with a rigidity in thinking."

My wife first said it during the presidential campaign debates, when issues emerged for which the programmers had not prepared Bush. "He's a dry drunk," she said, referring to the Alcoholics Anonymous term that describes the alcoholic who no longer drinks, but has not stopped thinking about drinking and has not entered a program to deal with his addiction.

Van Wormer, a professor of social work at the University of Northern Iowa and the co-author of *Addiction Treatment: A Strength's Perspective* (2002), says dry drunks tend "to go to extremes." I immediately thought about his religious fundamentalism, his insistence on an extreme tax plan, his threat to "smoke 'em out." As we all have heard, Bush called for a "crusade" after 9/11, which he later rescinded, but he loves to label his enemies as evil. Van Wormer also lists "exaggerated self-importance and grandiose behavior" as characteristics of dry drunks. Judge for yourselves!

Arguably the least-qualified president, Bush presides over the most complicated period of world history. The American economy needs a public that stays in a constant shopping frenzy. That requires certain kinds of freedom: freedom for advertisers to produce desire and then to confuse it with need. Commodity peddlers need broad freedom to lure anxious customers into purchasing goods and services to allegedly elevate their status, self-esteem, sexual prowess, and power, as well as to improve or enhance their body features. In *Upside Down: A Primer for the Looking-Glass World* (2001), Eduardo Galeano calls advertisers those who "know how to turn merchandise into magic charms against loneliness. Things have human attributes: they caress, accompany, understand, help. Perfume kisses you, your car never lets you down."

The car, or SUV, has become a basic capital good, which our system must mass produce. The very act of producing gas-burning vehicles, however, conflicts with the future of human life on the planet: global warming, ozone layer depletion, and so on. Bush's policies exacerbate the environmental issue. Instead of confronting this reality, Bush and his followers pray that the end will soon come. Perhaps his troublesome teenage twins make him feel desperate and thus contribute to his desire to bring it all to an end.

My teenager finishes her greasy burger, belches, and does not sing great songs about Bush.

May 2003

6

Closing Remarks

There Is Life after Shopping—
and It Feels Good

College bred men should be agitators to tear a question open and
riddle it with light and educate the moral sense of the masses.
—Wendell Phillips, quoted in Richard Hofstadter's
The American Political Tradition

Ask not what your country can do for you; ask what you can do for
your country.
—John F. Kennedy's January 1961 Inaugural Address

Philosophers have only interpreted the world in various ways; the
point is to change it.
—Karl Marx, *Theses on Feuerbach*

When a student asked me about the practical use of critical thinking for
her career in apparel market management, I shrugged my shoulders.

"I can't think of how you could apply Marx or Rousseau's texts to the
purchase of women's underwear or blouses," I responded. "But why take
a class in critical thinking to advance your marketing career?" I naively
asked.

She smiled. "I guess I want to learn something."

Her ambivalence reflects a large sector of the student population who
attend college as students used to go to vocational school: to learn a trade
or apprentice for a career. Instead of going to vocational high schools to
absorb the basics of auto mechanics or needle trades, students now
major in marketing or public relations, a field in the "communications"
major.

So, I asked my class after a discussion in which they had to compare
The Great Gatsby as novel and film, "What's the last thought you'll
have, 'darn it, I didn't get that extra-souped-up Porsche or I participated
in the making of history during my lifetime?'"

Some students stared at me in disbelief, others chuckled, and a few
looked down. I didn't expect an answer. As we left the classroom, one

young woman said, "Thanks, I needed that. I'm getting sick of so-called practical education. It might prepare you to enter the corporate ranks, but it doesn't prepare you to become a citizen, a parent, or a real person. But how else can you compete in the rat race?"

I thought of Lily Tomlin's remark. "The trouble with being in the rat race is that even if you win, you're still a rat."

Not everyone, however, has "bought" into the commercial culture. The tens of millions worldwide who took to the streets to protest against Bush's Iraq war, the tens of thousands who continue to demonstrate at meetings of the WTO, IMF, and the World Bank, institutions that symbolize the economic inequities perpetuated by corporate globalization (capitalism in its twenty-first century form), have become actors in their own historical drama. They consciously opt, some for an occasional day, for political agitation over shopping or "security."

These same people received the "normal" conditioning apparatus that teaches children to demand constant visual and audio stimulation that suggests shopping as a cure for all ills, and that beats "inadequacy" as a constant state of being into the minds of viewers and listeners. Such taming of the human spirit begins when the mother turns on the TV for the child. It continues on throughout one's life.

Those who rebel against the shopping experience as the American way of life must reject the core of messages they receive on TV and radio, spam on the Internet, massive amounts of print advertisements as part of "your newspaper," billboards, and the ever lurking vending machines.

Each piece of technology adds to the distraction of the citizen. The labor-saving device sold as a toy or adult play gadget—cell phones, laptops, Palm Pilots, and the like—change, once again, people's relationship to time and space. Think of the ever-increasing expectations for speed in reaching the Internet. People now complain of a twelve-hour plane flight from California to Europe as "an eternity," whereas seventy years ago one would spend two weeks on a ship to reach the same destination.

The new technology also further diverts the brain from organic reflection, from critical thinking, into narrow mind patterns related to technological efficiency. The speed with which life patterns have changed over the last forty years constitutes a kind of revolution, one that has not redistributed wealth or provided justice, but has contributed to the further marginalization of people as citizens.

To advocate Luddism is both impractical and beside the point. Technology, once invented, does not simply disappear. Indeed, Marx referred to it as a force of production. The point made by the Zapatista Army of

National Liberation in their January 1, 1994 Chiapas uprising is that pre-industrial societies could use post-industrial technology to promote their own survival.

Indeed, the Mayan Indians chose that day for their rebellion because it coincided with the implementation of NAFTA, the North American Free Trade Agreement. The Zapatistas argued that "free trade" policies would lead to the death of the indigenous people. They bolstered their case by pointing to President Salinas' 1991 revision of Article 27 of the Mexican Constitution. Salinas, fearing that the *ejido*, or collectively held land that could not be sold, rented, or leased, would repel foreign investors; so, to prepare Mexico for entry into NAFTA, he repealed the guarantees for holding communal land.

The indigenous people also correctly predicted that subsidized US agribusiness would drive the marginal corn-producing Indians of Mexico's south off their land and convert them into parts of the growing new world proletarian army. In this process they would lose not only their historic land, but their entire history and thus their identity.

Mexico, once known for its self-sufficiency in corn and beans, has become one of the major importers of both of those staples, from US agribusiness, of course. The economic avalanche, the Zapatistas warned, would produce a cultural one as well. Indeed, modern Mexico is filled, as are many third-world countries, with US-based chain-store outlets, many of them located at newly built malls.

The Zapatista revolt sounded the alarm for other indigenous people facing similar challenges to their cultural survival. Using the Internet to spread their word, the Zapatista cause as articulated by the witty Subco-mandante Marcos, resonated in Tibet and in parts of Africa as well as with indigenous people throughout the western hemisphere.

Those who believed with Marcos that the world would be poorer without the diversity of cultures understood that globalization's pro-moters desired a world of producers and consumers, with no place in it for Mayans or Tibetans.

The 1994 Chiapas uprising signaled a new wave of activism, a new feeling of hope and possibility. The fact that poorly armed Indians could capture eight municipalities and hold them even for a few days in Mexico inspired opponents of the new world order.

Those who campaigned on university campuses against sweatshops and child labor, for justice for low-paid US workers and for immigrant rights, came together with the enemies of the elite "free trade" bodies. At Harvard, "justice for janitors" became a major cause, and the students successfully won the demands for decent wages and conditions. At other universities similar movements emerged.

A new consciousness about the world led to the emergence in the late 1990s of a new opposition to corporate globalization, one that borrowed from Marxism but rejected Marx's idea that "man should conquer Nature." Indeed, environmentalism became the parchment on which the diverse opposition groups wrote their demands. The new movement does not rely on leaders or try to curry favor with the corrupt and manipulative media. They did what they had to do to make the statements they had to make about conditions in their time. They made history.

It is a tribute to the critical capacity of the human spirit that so many millions have discarded the superficial—albeit very acceptable if not downright patriotic—demands to conform and have declared their intention to participate in a historical process informed with the values of equality and justice.

Some of the 1999 Seattle protestors told me they were revolutionaries. Many of these same people stalked the nonelected elite who sit on boards of the WTO and advise the G-8 as they determine world economic policies. The economic heavies now meet in remote enclaves to attempt to rid themselves of those annoying protestors.

The protestors, organizing largely through the Internet, faced at each demonstration a brutal police presence, endured beatings and arrests and came back for more.[1]

Many were the same age or just a bit older than my students. They were revolutionaries, but not the ones that Marx envisioned who would bring in a socialist replacement for capitalism. "For Marx," wrote Walter Benjamin, "revolutions were the locomotives of history. But things have changed. Maybe revolutions become the means, that humanity, which rides on the train, employs to pull the emergency brake."[2]

Throughout history human beings have struggled for more justice and equality. In the modern era, the conscious actors will add the very survival of the planet as a place compatible with human life. So much is at stake and the best and the brightest have left the comfort zone to do battle.

Notes

Introduction

1. *Anderson Valley Advertiser*, July 23, 2002.
2. In a 1995 Washington paper, Martha Honey, a fellow at the Washington DC Institute for Policy Studies (IPS), wrote an investigative report documenting the existence of domestic "slavery" by some of Washington's most privileged international civil servants and described a "modern-day Underground Railroad," a loose network of churches, social service groups, lawyers, and individuals, quietly helping scores of domestic workers escape exploitative and often abusive situations, get legal help, and find other employment. According to IPS' Campaign for Domestic Worker Rights Project,

    > Most of these domestic workers are poor women from developing countries in Africa, Asia and Latin America who come to the U.S. (mainly Washington and New York) on special A-3 and G-5 visas, to work in the homes of diplomats and officials of the World Bank, International Monetary Fund (IMF), United Nations, and other international organizations.

    See "Empowering the Powerless: The Campaign for Migrant Domestic Worker Rights," available online at <http://www.ips-dc.org/campaign/article.htm>.
3. On January 1, 1994, the day Mexico entered the North American Free Trade Agreement the primarily indigenous Zapatista Army of National Liberation (EZLN) staged an armed uprising in the southeastern Mexican state of Chiapas, with rebels taking over the municipalities of San Cristóbal de las Casas, Ocosingo, Las Margaritas, Altamirano, Chanal, Oxchuc, and Huixtan and demanding democracy, liberty, and justice for all Mexicans. The EZLN's General Command issued the First Declaration of the Lacandon Jungle, demanding an end to "500 years of struggle" and declaring the Mexican Federal Army "the pillar of the Mexican dictatorship that we suffer from, monopolized by a one-party system and led by Carlos Salinas de Gortari, the maximum and illegitimate federal executive that today holds power." After almost two weeks of heavy fighting, the Salinas government declared a ceasefire on January 12, honored by the EZLN. See Joshua Paulson's "Chronological History of the Dialogue between the EZLN and the Mexican Government,

1994–1998," available online at <http://www.ezln.org/archivo/fzln/time-line.html>.

1. The Bush Vision

1. Morse, David. "What was behind the Pentagon's betting parlor?" *Counterpunch*, August 5, 2003. Available online at <http://www.counterpunch.org/morse08052003.html>.
2. Borger, Julian. "Study of Bush's psyche touches a nerve," *The Guardian*, August 13, 2003. According to Borger, "A study funded by the US government has concluded that conservatism can be explained psychologically as a set of neuroses rooted in 'fear and aggression, dogmatism and the intolerance of ambiguity.'" The authors also peer into the psyche of President George Bush, who turns out to be a textbook case. The telltale signs are his preference for moral certainty and frequently expressed dislike of nuance.
3. On July 28, 2003, J.P. Morgan Chase & Co. and Citigroup reached an agreement that includes, according to Ben White and Peter Behr of *The Washington Post*,

   > The agreement includes $255 million in payments to settle cases brought by the Securities and Exchange Commission and $50 million to settle allegations lodged by the Manhattan district attorney's office. The charges cover some $8.5 billion that Enron raised through complicated offshore transactions with the banks in the six years before its collapse in late 2001.

   See "Banks Will Pay for Enron Role." Available online at <http://www.yourlawyer.com/practice/news.htm?story_id=6376&topic=Enron%20Stock%20Fraud>.
4. The California Three Strikes Law went into effect in March 1994. According to an analysis by the RAND organization,

   > although the first two 'strikes' accrue for serious felonies, the crime that triggers the life sentence can be any felony. Furthermore, the law doubles sentences for a second strike, requires that these extended sentences be served in prison (rather than in jail or on probation), and limits 'good time' earned during prison to 20 percent of the sentence given (rather than 50 percent, as under the previous law).

   See "California's New Three Strikes Law: Benefits, Costs and Alternatives. Available online at <http://www.rand.org/publications/RB/RB4009/RB4009.word.html>.
5. See Robert Manning's book, *Credit Card Nation*, Basic Books, 2000, for a comprehensive look at America's addiction to credit cards.

2. Classify This!

1. Padilla, a US citizen, was originally held in the custody of the US Justice Department as a "material witness" and given access to an attorney after being arrested on May 8, 2002 on suspicion for allegedly

conspiring to detonate a radioactive "dirty bomb" in a US city. He was transferred to military custody on June 9, 2002 after President Bush designated him to be an "enemy combatant" associated with Al Qaeda. Since then, according to a June 11, 2003 Amnesty International press release (AI INDEX: AMR 51/084/2003), Padilla "has been held incommunicado in US military custody for a year without charge or trial…and without access to an attorney or to his family in a navy jail in Charleston, South Carolina." The press release also notes, "An appeal by the US government is currently pending against a US district court's order that Jose Padilla be given access to his lawyer." The press release is available online at <http://web.amnesty.org/library/Index/ENGAMR 510842003?open&of=ENG-2M4>.

2. According to the March 24, 2002 *Observer* ("I was Tortured by US Troops, Says Taliban American" (<http://observer.guardian.co.uk/print/0,3858,4380539-102275,00.html>), Lindh's lawyers claimed that he was systematically brutalized and threatened with "torture and death" after he was taken into custody by US troops following his November 24, 2001 surrender to the Northern Alliance. For several hours, according to the defense, " 'He was held in a room in which the only window was blocked, making it difficult to discern whether it was night or day,' " the lawyers said, adding that he was fed sparingly and given only minimal medical attention. After being transferred to Camp Rhino, the US base near Kandahar, " 'He was blindfolded and bound with plastic cuffs so tight they cut off the circulation to his hands. Mr. Lindh's clothes were cut off, his hands and feet were again shackled and he was bound tightly with duct tape to a stretcher. Still blindfolded and naked, he was placed in a metal shipping container.' " Adds the *Observer*, he was taken to a building or tent, where he was met by an FBI agent. The defense noted that " 'Mr. Lindh believed the only way to escape the torture was to do whatever the agent wanted.' "

On April 12, 2002, *CNN.com* reported that the Pentagon found more photos of US Special Forces in Afghanistan posing with blindfolded and shackled Lindh. A previously released photo used by Lindh's defense team showed Lindh naked on a stretcher, blindfolded, and handcuffed. Ultimately, Lindh pleaded guilty on July 15, 2002, to one charge of supplying services to the Taliban and another charge of carrying explosives. Under the plea deal, according to the July 15 *ABC News.com*, he will "serve two consecutive 10-year prison sentences and provide U.S. authorities with any information in their investigation of Al Qaeda and other terrorist groups." See " 'American Taliban' Pleads Guilty," available online at <http://observer. guardian.co.uk/international/story/0,6903,672986,00.html>.

3. Sheep Don't Need Whipping

1. According to an Associated Press story by Naomi Koppel ("Programs to Help Poor Nations Criticized," July 08, 2003), the United Nations Development Program's 2003 Human Development Report found that

international programs to help poor nations develop and industrialize are "failing in many countries and need radical changes if the world is to meet its targets for reducing poverty." Specifically, the report called on the IMF and World Bank to be "pressing rich countries to provide more help," instead of forcing developing countries to cut back on public spending. In poverty-stricken Africa, the report cited the case of Malawi, which has acceded to IMF and World Bank guidelines for reducing poverty. However, according to the report, "Malawi requires far more donor assistance—as do many other countries in similar circumstances." The article is available online at <http://www.globalexchange.org/campaigns/wbimf/770.html.pf>.

2. Mad Dog Productions, Inc. The quote appears online at <http://www.maddogproductions.com/ds_buying_votes.htm>.

3. *2002 Junk Food News List* is available online at <http://www.projectcensored.org>.

4. Quote available online at <http://www.uiowa.edu/~cyberlaw/tpfl/tpflch03. html>.

5. Quote available online at <http://www.thinkexist.com/English/Author/x/Author_4807_2.htm>

6. Quote available online at <http://www.brainyquote.com/quotes/quotes/d/davidfrost122844.html>.

7. Quote available online at <http://www.brainyquote.com/quotes/quotes/g/gorevidal103713.html>.

8. Quote available online at <http://www.brainyquote.com/quotes/quotes/a/annlanders108075.html>.

9. Hanna, in Max Frisch's Homo Faber, "Second Stop," Harvest Books, 1994.

10. On July 16, 2003, the House Appropriations Committee, by a 40 to 25 bipartisan vote, approved a provision that would undo the FCC's new rule that allows a single company to own more TV stations in the same market and expand its collective reach of US households to forty-five percent. In the House, a bipartisan group of senators pressed ahead with their own legislative effort to derail the FCC's new regulations. *Online News Hour*, PBS, July 18, 2003, "Congress Gains Momentum in Effort to Overturn FCC Rules." Available online at <http://www.pbs.org/newshour/media/media_watch/july-dec03/fcc_7–16.html>.

11. Quote available online at <http://www.comedy.com/jokes/cjod_past.asp>.

4. Ahab Can Beat the Whale

1. Quote available online at <http://warren.dusd.net/~dstone/Resources/11P/Emerson01.htm>.

2. Quote available online at <http://www.angelfire.com/retro/cyclone/movement.htm>.

3. Quote available online at <http://www.brainyquote.com/quotes/quotes/a/alberteins141508.html>.

4. Quote available online at <http://www.armory.com/~mrlinux/wisdom. html>.

5. Quote available online at <http://www.brainyquote.com/quotes/quotes/ w/willrogers109468.html >.

6. Quote available online at <http://www.allspirit.co.uk/emerson.html# rhodora>.

7. Quote available online at <http://www.brainyquote.com/quotes/ quotes/t/tallulahba141936.html>.

8. Quote available online at <http://www.quotegallery.com/asp/ apcategories.asp?author=Woody+Allen>.

9. Quote available online at <http://www.brainyquote.com/quotes/quotes/ w/woodyallen128351.html >.

10. Shanti Menon, "Sick of El Niño," February 16, 1998. Available at *<http://www.discoverer.com>*.

11. According to the United Nations Development Program's 2003 Human Development Report, in the 1990s, "the average per capita income growth was less than 3 percent in 125 developing and transition countries and in 54 of them the average per capita income fell" (page 3). The report also notes that "more than 1.2 billion people—1 in every 5 on Earth—survive on less than one dollar a day" (page 5). Report available online at *<http://www.undp.org/hdr2003/pdf>*.

12. Quote available online at <http://www.bartleby.com/63/73/2373.html>.

13. Quote available online at <http://www.brainyquote.com/quotes/ quotes/g/gorevidal112500.html>.

14. Quote available online at <http://www.brainyquote.com/quotes/quotes/ r/robertorbe104953.html>.

15. page 1, Chapter 1, Harper Collins, New York.

16. According to the March 28, 2003 BBC, "The controversy centres on Mr. Perle's deal with Global Crossing to win US Government approval of its proposed partial sale to Asian investors, from which Mr. Perle stood to make hundreds of thousands of dollars." See "Top US hawk Perle resigns," available online at <http://news.bbc.co.uk/2/hi/americas/ 2894059.stm>. For a look at another related controversy surrounding Perle, his meeting with Adnan Khashoggi, see Seymour Hersh's profile in the March 17, 2003 *New Yorker*, "Lunch with the Chairman."

5. The Iraq Conundrum

1. John Frisbee, "The Mayaguez Incident," *Air Force Magazine*, Vol. 74, No. 9, September 1991.

2. According to the November/December 1991 FAIR report, "Inside Bohemian Grove: The Story *People Magazine* Won't Let you Read,"

   Bohemian Grove, a secluded campground in California's Sonoma County, is the site of an annual two-week gathering of a highly select, all-male club, whose members have included every Republican president since Calvin Coolidge. Current participants include George Bush, Henry Kissinger, James Baker and David Rockefeller—a virtual who's who of the most powerful men in business and government.

See Report online at <http://www.fair.org/extra/best-of-extra/bohemian-grove.html>.

3. A May 2003 BBC investigative report concluded, Lynch's "story is one of the most stunning pieces of news management ever conceived." As Robert Scheer reports in his May 20, 2003 *Los Angeles Times* column, "Saving Private Lynch: Take 2,"

> It has since emerged that Lynch was neither shot nor stabbed, but rather suffered accident injuries when her vehicle overturned. A medical checkup by U.S. doctors confirmed the account of the Iraqi doctors, who said they had carefully tended her injuries, a broken arm and thigh and a dislocated ankle, in contrast to U.S. media reports that doctors had ignored Lynch.

4. October 15, 2002 "No Fly" List Online Complaint Form:

> Have you been barred from flying because of your political views? The ACLU wants to hear from you. Federal Officials have given airlines a blacklist of people to prevent from flying because they are deemed suspicious. Sure, terrorists shouldn't fly, but government has to be accountable for the fairness of the list. Already there are reports of people being stopped at airports because of their lawful political activity. The ACLU wants to hear from anyone who has been barred from flying because of their political views.

5. In 2003, Miramax re-released *The Quiet American* for a short time. Actor Michael Caine was nominated for an Academy Award.

6. Closing Remarks

1. At the 2001 Genoa G-8 protests, over 600 protestors were injured and one was killed by Italian police. According to a statement released by five Britons held by Italian police after the protest, "Police indiscriminately batoned those present, mainly young people offering no resistance." See "G-8 Britons tell of Police 'Brutality,'" *BBC News*, July 26, 2001. Available online at <http://news.bbc.co.uk/1/hi/uk/1457920.stm>.

2. *On the Concept of History, Thesis 6*, quoted in Adolfo Gilly "El Siglo de Relampago," page 19, La Jornada ediciones, 2002, Mexico.

Bibliography

Alterman, Eric. *What Liberal Media? The Truth About Bias and the News.* New York: Basic, 2003.

Berger, John. *Ways of Seeing.* London, UK: BBC-Penguin, 1972.

Berger, John, and Mohr, Jean. *Another Way of Telling.* New York: Pantheon, 1982.

Gutman, Herbert G. *Power & Culture: Essays on the American Working Class.* New York: Pantheon, 1987.

Hofstadter, Richard. *The American Political Tradition.* New York: Vintage, 1954.

Huffington, Arianna. *Pigs at the Trough: How Corporate Greed and Political Corruption Are Undermining America.* New York: Crown, 2003.

Linker, Kate. *Love for Sale: The Words and Picture of Barbara Kruger.* New York: Abrams, 1990.

Mander, Jerry. *Four Arguments for the Elimination of Television.* New York: Morrow, 1978.

Manning, Robert D. *Credit Card Nation.* New York: Basic, 2000.

Mills, C. Wright. *The Sociological Imagination.* New York: Oxford University Press, 2000.

Postman, Neil. *Amusing Ourselves to Death: Public Discourse in the Age of Show Business.* New York: Penguin, 1985.

Raskin, Marcus G. *Liberalism: The Genius of American Ideals.* Lanham, MD: Rowman & Littlefield, 2003.

Schechter, Danny. *The More You Watch, The Less You Know.* New York: Seven Stories Press, 1997.

Schiller, Herb. *Culture, Inc.: The Corporate Takeover of Public Expression.* New York: Oxford, 1989.

———. *Information Inequality: The Deepening Social Crisis in America.* New York: Routledge, 1996.

———. *Mass Communications and American Empire.* New York: Augustus M. Kelley, 1969, Rev ed. 1992.

Vidal, Gore, *Perpetual War for Perpetual Peace?* Nation, 2002.

———. *Dreaming War: Blood for Oil and the Cheney-Bush Junta.* Nation, 2002.

West, Nathanael. *The Day of the Locust.* New York: Signet Classics, 1983.

Web Sites

Common Dreams: <http://www.commondreams.org>
Counterpunch: <http://www.counterpunch.org>
Institute for Policy Studies (IPS): <http://www.ips-dc.org>
Not in Our Name: <http://www.notinourname.net>
Progreso Weekly: <http://www.progresoweekly.com>
The Nation: <http://www.thenation.com>
The Progressive: <http://www.progressive.org>
Tom Paine:< http://www.tompaine.com>
Transnational Institute (TNI): <http://www.tni.org>
Z Mag: <http://www.zmag.org>

Index